"Fr. Younan's foray into w
is both entertaining and
good deal of time engagin~
Not only can he articulate their objections (in ...,
them) better than they can, but he provides sound reason in
response. And reason and rationality are at the heart of his
presentation. Thanks for bringing Thomas Aquinas' own
clarity back to the fore."

—MOST REV. EARL BOYEA
Bishop of the Diocese of Lansing

"*Thoughtful Theism* is one of the best responses to the New
Atheism I have ever read. Fr. Younan writes in a lively manner
that will have special appeal to young adults. He examines
the arguments of the New Atheists with philosophical skill
and linguistic precision. He exposes many straw men, false
dichotomies, and unsubstantiated assertions in authors like
Dawkins and Krauss, and he makes a very strong case that
the atheists, not the theists, are the ones who are really irrational. Drawing heavily upon St. Thomas Aquinas, Fr.
Younan challenges theists to use sound reason in support
of faith. He shows that the existence of God is not at all
threatened by the Big Bang, evolution, or the existence of
evil. *Thoughtful Theism* is a great resource for those wishing
to respond to aggressive atheism in an informed and rational manner."

—ROBERT FASTIGGI, PH.D.
Professor of Systematic Theology,
Sacred Heart Major Seminary

"In this book, Fr. Younan carries out philosophy's Socrat-
ic vocation of helping young minds to overcome sophist-
ry and to transform mere opinion into knowledge. In this
case, the aim is the all-important goal of knowing the ex-

istence of God by the light of natural reason. Fr. Younan sets out the classic arguments for the existence of God and with scrupulous fairness examines and rebuts the objections offered by the New Atheists and their contemporary allies. He does this with wit and a conversational style that makes this challenging material readily accessible to those who are coming new to the effort. *Thoughtful Theism* is a solid resource for the work of dispelling from our contemporary pseudo-sophisticated culture the fog of unbelief."

—MOST. REV. ALLEN H. VIGNERON,
Archbishop of the Archdiocese of Detroit

"In this engaging book, Fr. Andrew Younan offers hope and encouragement to believers who may be upset, disheartened, angry or simply confused by the barrage of books and arguments coming from the New Atheists. With something like the fervor of a personal trainer, Fr. Younan presents his basic message that belief in God is reasonable. He encourages his readers to think for themselves and not be intimidated by atheists. He admits that 'thinking is hard work' and gives us a lot to think about through his pointed rebuttal of the atheists, his careful explanations of arguments for the existence of God (including those of St. Thomas Aquinas), and his lucid account of the harmony of faith and contemporary science (including Big Bang cosmology and evolutionary biology). His book is a tonic for all who would like to think more deeply about their faith in God."

—MICHAEL J. DODDS, O.P.
Professor of Philosophy & Theology,
Dominican School of Philosophy & Theology

Thoughtful Theism

REDEEMING REASON *in an* IRRATIONAL AGE

Thoughtful Theism

REDEEMING REASON
in an IRRATIONAL AGE

FR. ANDREW YOUNAN

EMMAUS
ROAD
PUBLISHING

Steubenville, Ohio
www.EmmausRoad.org

Emmaus Road Publishing
1468 Parkview Circle
Steubenville, Ohio 43952

Library of Congress Cataloging-in-Publication Data

Names: Younan, Andrew, 1979- author.
Title: Thoughtful theism: redeeming reason in an irrational age / Fr. Andrew
    Younan.
Description: Steubenville : Emmaus Road Pub., 2017.
Identifiers: LCCN 2017002998 (print) | LCCN 2017005204 (ebook) | ISBN
    9781945125324 (hardcover) | ISBN 9781945125331 (pbk.) | ISBN 9781945125348
    (ebook)
Subjects: LCSH: Faith and reason--Christianity. | Christianity and atheism. |
    Atheism. | Theism.
Classification: LCC BT50 .Y68 2017 (print) | LCC BT50 (ebook) | DDC
    261.2/1--dc23
LC record available at https://lccn.loc.gov/2017002998

Cover design and layout by Margaret Ryland
Cover image used under license from Triff / Shutterstock.com

For anyone wondering what's going on.

"I love him who lives to know."

—Nietzsche
(*Thus Spoke Zarathustra*, First Part, Prologue, 4)

TABLE OF CONTENTS

Acknowledgments

For what it's worth, I'd like to thank my parents: my dad for never letting me put reason aside for faith, and my mom for showing me how to keep my faith through everything. My siblings also, Chris and Kristina, for showing me how to be myself and how to never give up, each in their own way. I owe great gratitude to many mentors and friends whose constant insights and challenges have formed me more than I could ever express: Bishop Sarhad Jammo of the Chaldean Church, Archbishop Allen Vigneron of Detroit, Dr. John Goyette of Thomas Aquinas College, Fr. Michael Dodds of the D.S.P.T., and Fr. Francis Dobrzenski of the U.P. I owe a great deal to John Paul the Great Catholic University, especially to Dr. Derry and Lidy Connolly, my colleagues in "the Thinkery:" Drs. Michael Barber, John Kincaid, Matthew Peterson, and Tom Harmon, as well as all the students that have kept me on my toes all these years. Finally, I thank the seminarians of Mar Abba the Great and the Workers of the Vineyard convent for trying their best to keep me human and sane, despite my best efforts; all the friends who have looked at earlier manuscripts of this book and given valuable feedback; a little boy named Jason; and a nameless little girl.

BAGHDAD, CALIFORNIA

One of the best things about multiculturalism is the food. In San Diego, where I live, you can get some of the best fish tacos and falafel in the world. I hate both. But you can also get California Burritos and Sahara Fries. If you don't know what a California Burrito is, I feel very sad for you. It's a burrito filled with carne asada (basically chopped steak), french fries, sour cream, and cheese. It will change your life forever. Sahara Fries are harder to find, but they are also french fries, but this time covered with shawarma meat and some sauce that makes you cry with joy when you consume it. The best products of multiculturalism are when cultures meld. Overpriced restaurants call this "fusion," but I doubt it has anything to do with the nuclei of atoms.

Some things in every culture are good, like carne asada and shawarma. Some things are bad, like falafel and fish tacos. The way to tell the difference is through reason— the exercise of our minds. That's what this book is basically about. Obviously, food is a matter of taste. That's pretty much the definition of "taste," so if you happen to like falafel or fish tacos, don't be offended. I don't think you're evil or wrong. I just think you have bad taste, and only started this book by talking about food because I was hungry and figured it might work as a symbol. But some things aren't a matter of taste. Whether or not there is a

God (the main question of this book), is not a matter of taste, and when you disagree with someone on this question, you're not disagreeing about what you like or dislike. One of you is wrong.

Of course, being wrong doesn't mean one person is worth less than someone else. That's something that (I hope) all reasonable people can agree on. Unfortunately, I'm not sure how common reasonable people are these days. My second cousin was, up until a year ago, the Archbishop of Mosul, Iraq for the Chaldean Catholic Church (if you don't know who Chaldeans are, they are the Aramaic-speaking indigenous people of Iraq, and most are Christian). I remember visiting Iraq for the first (and, probably, last) time with my parents in 2014, a few months before ISIS became a thing (at least a thing with a name), and seeing this Archbishop cousin of mine there. Even then, Mosul was too dangerous to visit, so he met us in Erbil, and told us he was rapidly losing his Church. A few months after our visit, there were no Christians left in the Archdiocese of Mosul, and my second cousin was transferred to Australia to serve the Chaldeans who live there. He will very likely be the last Archbishop of Mosul. Oh, and his predecessor, Archbishop Paulos Faraj Rahho, was martyred in 2008. Like I said, I'm not sure how common reasonable people are these days.

The title of this book is *Honest to God: Thoughtful Theism in an Irrational Age*. The purpose of the book is to show that belief in God is a reasonable thing. This purpose, however, has two types of opponents: one is represented by ISIS and groups like it (by no means monopolized by Islam). The way they oppose is by deleting the "thoughtful" and using "theism" as an instrument for evil. I'm not sure a book is the best way to deal with that problem. Another group of opponents says that theism is unreasonable as an intellectual concept, and attempts to show this through writing and debate. A group who does this, on whom I focus in this book, is popularly called the "New Atheists." Their most notable authors are Richard Dawkins, Christopher Hitchens, Lawrence Krauss, Daniel Denett, and Sam Harris (there are also a handful of others I refer to in this book—for a decently thorough list see the bibliography). I don't think this group of writers is made up of bad people. In fact, whether they are good or bad isn't my business at all. But I do think they're wrong. I am grateful, however, that they and I can discuss a question like this, disagree with each other, and not threaten or kill one another.

It seems to me that the heart of the cultural conflict we face today is not between religions, or between religion and irreligion. It seems that the heart of the conflict we have always faced as human beings is between rationality and irrationality. This book is an attempt to take a step toward rationality, and to show that rationality and theism go together hand in hand.

CHAPTER ONE

CALM DOWN

"Science has disproven God."

"Evolution shows that the origin and development of life requires no intelligent design."

"Religion is a human invention created to keep people obedient and passive."

"Belief in God has caused countless acts of violence and evil in the world."

"Your holy book is utterly man-made and filled with all kinds of error and ignorance."

"If God made the world, then who made God?"

Ask yourself if you've been in this situation before: someone with a differing belief confronts you, they are more well-read on the subject, they bombard you with questions or statements you can't answer, you feel incompetent and begin to have serious doubts about what you believe.

If you're the type of person who routinely avoids this kind of confrontation, or who finds it distasteful or awkward, I challenge you to question yourself as well as your beliefs. Being challenged about an opinion or belief is not a bad thing; quite the contrary, it is one of the few things on earth powerful enough to get an ordinarily complacent, even lazy, human being to do the one thing he or she was ultimately meant to do: think.

The Divided Line (Look It Up)

Thinking is hard work. That's why, if I can make a mean generalization, so few people do it. Believing is, in itself, pretty easy, though oftentimes the consequences of belief can be deeply challenging. Having an opinion is the easiest thing of all. *Thinking* is the process whereby our minds attempt to arrive at a true understanding of reality, which, if successful, leads to *knowledge* ("I know there is ice at the South Pole"). *Believing* is affirming something about reality. It can (and should) be the result of thinking as well, to the greatest degree possible ("I believe that Jesus rose from the dead"). Having an *opinion* is affirming something about yourself ("My favorite color is red"). There's nothing hard there, unless perhaps you have a bad opinion of *Citizen Kane and express that opinion at a film school.*

Belief stands between opinion and knowledge, and can be pulled in one direction or another depending on the person and on the belief (I didn't come up with any of this, by the way—I got it from Plato's *Republic* Book VI). A belief with reasonable justification but no strict proof is closer to knowledge; a belief that is believed with no reason at all is practically the same as an opinion. This is simply to say that there are things about reality that might be difficult or impossible to prove completely one way or another, but that can be argued about and supported with evidence. The realm of belief is more like a court case than a mathematical proof, but that doesn't mean it is detached from reason completely. On the contrary, a true court case abounds with reasons and evidence, and the jury is challenged to think as honestly as they can about their verdict. But the fact is most court cases aren't utterly black and white, and the evidence must be examined carefully when there is no absolute proof that caught the defendant red-handed.

The question that is the topic of this book is about the existence of God. Does God exist, in reality, aside from any belief or opinion, as a knowable fact that can be arrived at through correct thinking? If you're paying attention, you'll realize that this is really two questions: Is there a God, and can we know there is a God? I'm going to focus on the first question. If we can arrive at a positive answer for it (a clear yes or no), then the second question is answered. If not, then the second question will need its own attention, and we can ask whether we can "know" there is or is not a God, or whether we can only "believe" either way, and which side has the most evidence, so that we have a belief justified with reasons and evidence, rather than a belief that is only a meagre opinion.

I Don't Care How You Feel

Of course, it's important to understand from the start that arriving at the truth is a matter of thinking, and not of feeling. That might sound impolite, but there's no way around it. You can feel with all your heart that there's a God near you at all times, or you can feel utterly abandoned and alone in the world, and the plain fact of the matter is that it doesn't make a difference. If there isn't a God, your feeling doesn't make him exist or prove that he does, and if there is one, he's there whether you like it or not, and no matter how alone you might feel.

Lawrence Krauss, one of the "New Atheism" authors I discuss in this book, makes this point nicely: "The existence or nonexistence of a creator is independent of our desires. A world without God or purpose may seem harsh or pointless, but that alone doesn't require God to actually exist."[1] Of course, I'd hold him (and anyone else in his school of thought) to the same standard, and expect him to admit there is a God if the argument holds, independently of what he would feel (or want) to be the case.

CALM DOWN I SAID

Here's the real problem, though: thinking isn't just hard work; it takes a lot of time and patience as well. There's a positive side to the bombardment I described above: it gets you to think and question the basis for your beliefs. But there's a negative side as well: when many questions are thrown together at once, it can imply that, if you can't answer them immediately, it means you're wrong. Even worse, it can imply that these questions can or should be answered quickly. Those are both awful implications.

The first implication is simply bad logic: "I asked you a question. You can't answer it right now. Therefore you are wrong." The logic might prove that you are ignorant, but it certainly doesn't prove that what you're saying is untrue. There could be ten million truths unknown to both your opponent and yourself; there could be a thousand different ways of interpreting things that neither of you have come up with. The truth of reality is not bound by your personal ability to argue or understand. Reality is what it is, independent of anyone's competence, and the real goal, if you are an honest person, is not to win an argument but to understand the world. This is one of the many reasons I despise most styles of debate. (You'll hear me complain about a lot of pet peeves throughout this book.)

---

[1] Lawrence Krauss, *A Universe from Nothing: Why There Is Something Rather than Nothing* (New York: Atria Trade Paperbacks, 2012), xxii.

The second implication is, like I said, worse. It implies that the truth of the world can be known easily and quickly, that a question as big as the existence of God can be resolved in a few hours or a handful of rhetorical jabs. This is not only insulting to the human mind as well as our amazing universe, it undoes the great good accomplished by asking questions in the first place: your opponent asked you a question and now you have the opportunity to think, but if the question is "answered" so quickly, then your opportunity for thinking is gone. This is simply another form of the same laziness you had before, and if you don't take the time (and it can take a LOT of time) to work through every step of the argument for yourself, you are simply trading one opinion for another.

The Lazy Agnostic

Of course, there is another option. You could simply give up. It might be tempting to look at the hundreds of books written about the existence of God (I have a dozen books from the New Atheism movement sitting on my desk as I type this), and look at the ridiculous number of articles, blogs, Facebook posts, Tweets, and YouTube comments, and simply conclude that there is no answer that we could ever know. There are just too many arguments, they are too hard to answer, there is too little evidence, and we simply can't know. After all, if there were a real answer that could be discovered, why would so many people, who seem to be so intelligent in many cases, completely disagree on such a fundamental question?

The result of this is to conclude that you are an "a-gnostic," which means a "non-knower." Isaac Newton wrote proofs for God's existence and commentaries on the Bible;

Stephen Hawking is (sometimes) an avowed atheist. Their personal authority becomes irrelevant to the question, and their arguments are tough reading to almost anyone. So maybe our best bet is to just wash our hands of the entire question.

Yes, the question is a hard one. That's exactly why it takes so much time and effort. But that doesn't mean it's an impossible one. Secondly, the fact that an intelligent man has a belief does not mean that it is an intelligent belief. In exactly the same way, the fact that a scientist has a belief doesn't mean that it is a scientific belief. There's a lot more to a human being than meets the eye, and someone can be brilliant in one area and make enormous mistakes in reasoning or leaps of logic in another area. This includes your parents, your pastor, and all of your teachers. This question is too big to be trusted to anyone but yourself. This has everything to do with you, and you have to trust that your own mind is capable of working through every side and of finding an answer if there is an answer that can be found. I'd be quite upset if anyone took this book to be something to be "believed" outright. It isn't meant to be anything more than a presentation of the argument from one perspective, which seems to me to be the right one. If there is anyone interested in showing me where I'm wrong, I'd be quite happy to consider it. In fact, it's exactly because of this that I've spent so much time reading the New Atheism crowd (as well as their predecessors, most notably Hume and Nietzsche, both of whom I teach in my classes). I confess that I haven't read any of the Theist responses to their books, and so I apologize in advance if this book is repetitive of any others.

In any case, unless you've done the work and examined both sides fairly, honestly, and thoroughly, and have proven (to yourself at least) that no side in this question has any rational evidence over and above the other, "agnostic" isn't a reasonable conclusion for you to make. It's a lazy one. Similarly, unless you've faced the objections of serious atheists, your theism is a belief that is more like opinion than it is like knowledge—it is a "blind faith," and you have no way of knowing whether your faith is true and that of anyone else is false, since they made the same leap with the same blindfold over their eyes. Finally, unless you have taken seriously the best (not the worst) arguments of the theists and answered them satisfactorily, your atheism is as blind an opinion as the faith of any Muslim, Jew, or Christian who has never questioned his beliefs.

Many Questions: Continue Calming Down

An important point I want to make in this chapter is this: there are many different questions that need to be asked about God, and they are all distinct from each other. People fall into logical black holes when they fail to understand this simple point. Proving that God exists is *not at all* the same as proving that he (assuming this is the proper pronoun to use) is omnipotent, or omniscient, or good, or even that there is one of him. These are all completely different questions, whose arguments may or may not be related. If I attempt to prove that God exists, that argument should be examined according to what it is attempting to do, not anything else. If that argument does not prove that there is one God, or that God is all-powerful, or anything else, *that is not a problem*. It never attempted to prove those things, and it is either confused or dishonest to pretend that it did, or that there is a problem with the proof because it doesn't prove everything all at once.

Anyone attempting a true examination of this question must face this reality honestly.

Unfortunately, there are many who don't. I quote the most popular of the New Atheism authors, Richard Dawkins, as an example. In his treatment of Thomas Aquinas's Five Proofs (a treatment which I will examine in detail in a later chapter), Dawkins makes this statement:

> Even if we allow the dubious luxury of arbitrarily conjuring up a terminator to an infinite regress and giving it a name, simply because we need one, there is absolutely no reason to endow that terminator with any of the properties normally ascribed to God: omnipotence, omniscience, goodness, creativity of design, to say nothing of such human attributes as listening to prayers, forgiving sins and reading innermost thoughts.[2]

It should not surprise you that on this point I agree completely with Richard Dawkins. Thomas's proofs for God's existence give us "absolutely no reason" to believe that God is omnipotent, omniscient, good, or anything else. But they were never *meant* to give us any reason for any of those things, though they might imply them, or develop into other arguments about them later. St. Thomas's Five Ways only attempt to prove that God exists. Nothing more than that—certainly nothing related to prayer or forgiveness, which are questions related to "revealed" religion and to supernatural theology, not at all to philosophy (to which I will limit myself in this book, and to which Aquinas limits himself in those initial questions of the *Summa*).

This point, that each of these questions is separate,

---

2   Richard Dawkins, *The God Delusion* (New York: Mariner, 2008), 101.

is easily illustrated by glancing at the titles for the first handful of "Questions" of the *Summa Theologica* of Thomas Aquinas:

- The Existence of God
- The Simplicity of God
- The Perfection of God
- Goodness
- The Goodness of God
- The Infinity of God
- The Being of God in Things
- The Immutability of God
- The Eternity of God
- The Unity of God

Each of these "Questions" (and they continue for thousands of pages) contains several "Articles," wherein each question is broken down into even smaller pieces. Then within each "Article," several "Objections" are first brought up from opposing viewpoints, so that as much as possible no argument is neglected. This is how a careful thinker proceeds. Richard Dawkins dismisses Thomas Aquinas after four pages, using arguments like the one I quoted above (as you will see in the next chapter). Before him, Bertrand Russell is honest enough to admit what he's doing: "To come to this question of the existence of God: it is a large and serious question, and if I were to attempt to deal with it in any adequate manner I should have to keep you here until Kingdom Come, so that you will have to excuse me if I deal with it in a somewhat summary fashion."[3]

---

[3] Bertrand Russell, "The Existence of God" in *Why I Am Not a Christian: And Other Essays on Religion and Related Subjects* (New York: Touchstone, 1957), 5.

"There is absolutely no reason to endow that terminator with any of the properties normally ascribed to God . . ." This is either a serious misunderstanding by Professor Dawkins or a serious deception. It is not my business to judge which it is, but the fact remains that, at what I would argue is *the* critical moment in his book (his examination of the strongest proofs for God's existence), Dawkins makes an enormous logical blunder, and builds the rest of the argument of his book on this blunder. This is a shaky foundation, and I am saddened to think of the thousands of people who have claimed to have abandoned their belief in God because of his books when this is the kind of reasoning representative of his thought.

This logical glitch is also representative of the intellectual laziness I discussed earlier, though it is certainly not limited to atheists. Where there are many questions to ask, we would be tempted to reduce them to only one. But that will get us nowhere. Someone taking the question seriously would break the questions down into the smallest logical units possible and answer one at a time, in the most logical order. More thoughtful atheists do this quite well, of course. They ask whether there is a God, and conclude that the answer is no. After that, there's no reason to ask whether God is all-powerful, or all-knowing, or good, or bad, or anything else. Nor is there any reason to even begin asking which religion might be "the right one," if there is no God. This is all quite reasonable. The question that is the topic of this book is that first one—is there a God? I will not attempt to answer any other question in this book, since this is the first and biggest one to ask. Once it is answered satisfactorily, then someone might move on to the next question, whatever that might be.

Clearing the Dust

I'll be the first to admit that it's an odd phenomenon that many people, of seemingly strong intelligence, who all seem to have the ability to reason quite well, can come up with completely opposing conclusions. They're all looking at the same evidence, supposedly, which happens to be, in the case of the question of God, the entire world. They're all, I assume, using the same instrument to come to their conclusion, namely, human reason. What's the problem, then?

It's one of two possibilities. Someone is either looking wrongly, or reasoning wrongly. The name given for this is "fallacy." It's possible to look at only a part of the relevant evidence, and it's possible to reason incorrectly, or "invalidly," from the evidence. In this chapter, I'll attempt to clear away as much of this dust as possible, so that we can reason more clearly in the following chapters.

Hitchens' Razor: It Cuts Both Ways

Christopher Hitchens is credited with popularizing an old Latin proverb, "What can be asserted without evidence can be dismissed without evidence." This has even come to be called "Hitchens' Razor." It is, of course, quite correct.

Another way of saying it is that if a claim is to be given merit, there must be a "because" backing it up. If it's just a conclusion alone, then it's not an argument, and it can be denied as easily as it was affirmed. Here are some examples:

> *Religion is man-made.*
> *The Bible is the Word of God.*
> *Man created God in his own image.*
> *God created man in his own image.*
> *Theists believe in God to give themselves security in a harsh world.*
> *Atheists disbelieve in God to give themselves license to do whatever they please.*

These are statements, not arguments. An argument requires a "why" or "because." It requires evidence or argumentation. Without this, any one of them can be validly answered with the opposite affirmation, and nothing else. For example:

Proposition: "Man created God in his own image."
Perfectly Valid Response: "No, he didn't."

This is a sufficient logical answer, because no reason was given in the first place. What can be asserted without evidence can be dismissed without evidence. Of course, the reason why this kind of thing passes for an argument is that it has a certain rhetorical power, and might often imply a reason without stating it. But the question of God is too big for rhetoric or implication. So don't fall for this, and don't be intimidated by it. Make your opponent state the reasons for their affirmation clearly and explicitly, and you'll find that their foundation is often weaker than they pretend.

OPINIONS: EVERYONE HAS ONE

I've seen the results of various surveys thrown around citing some percentage or another of scientists being theists or atheists. The general consensus of such surveys is that there is an overwhelming majority of scientists who are atheists. Assuming this is true (which might be arguable), it doesn't really prove anything about the existence of God. It might prove something about the state of academia or of graduate schools, but in the end it is an argument about opinions, not about reality. If you wish to see the weakness in this (and many) arguments, try stating the implied conclusion directly after it and see if it follows. "Many scientists do not believe in God; therefore there is no God." This is a weak piece of reasoning because there are a million factors between the opinion of these scientists and the reality (or unreality) of God's existence.

Of course, the other implication is that science itself has disproven God. This is an even larger logical leap. There are a million questions in-between that need to be answered before this implied conclusion can even be examined, the most important of which is, "Is the existence of God even a question that can be answered by science?" I will attempt to address this question in chapter four. But until all such questions are given a clear and definitive answer, this argument carries the same weight as any other survey: it is about the opinions of individuals, and nothing more.

BIG WORDS DON'T MAKE YOU SMART

Speaking of science, my favorite among the books associated with the New Atheism movement is Laurence Krauss's *A Universe from Nothing*. I like it, and Krauss's other books, for many reasons, but one big reason is that Krauss is quite good at explaining complicated scientific concepts in layman's terms. This is a difficult and relatively rare skill. I'm not the first person to notice that, very often, people use large words not to explain ideas but to hide the fact that they don't know what they're talking about. They scatter dust into the air to block their opponent's vision.

You have two options when this happens: feel intimidated and stupid and assume your opponent just knows more than you do, or be humble and honest enough to ask, "What do you mean by that?" The first route can be called the "Emperor's New Clothes Syndrome." In this case, you're one of the people in the crowd looking at your naked king, afraid to look stupid by saying something that seems obvious to you. The second is the only real way to knowledge. I repeat a point I made earlier, because I think it's too easy to forget: *you* are the one figuring this out, and if a word, a claim, or an argument doesn't make sense to you, then you owe it to yourself to ask for clarification. If you try to clarify it and it still doesn't make sense to you, don't rule out the possibility that it's simply a bad argument, and that your opponent is the problem, not you. And if your opponent does understand more, he or she should be able to explain it to your satisfaction.

Neither side of any debate I've encountered is innocent of using technical or evasive terms to hide their ignorance. Dawkins pokes fun at the term *consubstantial*, for example.[1] I'm not sure about the amount of effort he makes in testing to see if this term really is as empty as he believes, but the point is, in general, a valid one. Other times, words are thrown about not only to cover up but to intimidate. "Heresy" was one such word used by the Church for centu-

---

[1] Dawkins, *The God Delusion*, 54.

ries (though it simply translates as "error"). Today, words that carry intimidating weight include "delusion," "ignorance," "Middle Ages," "unscientific," and so on.

"BURDEN OF PROOF:" SAYING THIS MAKES YOU SOUND SMART

"Burden of proof" is another phrase that can be used to mask an empty concept or viewpoint, and it can be used this way on every side of any argument:

Believing in a supernatural being is an absurd claim; the burden of proof is on the theist.

Believing in a universe that came from nothing is inconceivable; the burden of proof is on the atheist.

These are both intellectual dodges, neither really answering anything. Saying that believing in a supernatural being is "absurd" is to assume that the argument is over before it has begun (this is sometimes called "circular reasoning"). In fact, if there is a God (which is exactly what we're arguing about), then it's not at all absurd to believe in one. Saying that a universe from nothing is "inconceivable" is to do the same thing. If it's true, and we can discover it, it isn't inconceivable.

Of course, this is not to mention at all the very relevant questions, "What do you mean by Supernatural?" and "What do you mean by Nothing?" It's quite possible that even these terms, which would seem quite commonplace to most of us, could be used as a mask to cover up a valid question rather than answer it. In fact, the bulk of the work of philosophical thinking (when it's done well) is in clarifying what exactly we mean by the terms we use, and the many philosophical mistakes come from misusing terms, or using a term in two or more different senses.

Ockham's Razor: Kind of Useful

Speaking of philosophy, another term that is thrown about with reckless abandon is "Ockham's Razor" (sometimes spelled "Occam's Razor," named after the Franciscan Friar William of Ockham). Put simply, Ockham's Razor implies that the simplest solution to a problem is generally the best. But there's a complexity in that very idea. Who is to say that the claim "the universe came from nothing" is more or less simple than the claim "the universe came from God?" Is it the number of terms that determines the simplicity of the claim? Is "nothing" simpler of a concept than "God?" And again, how are either of these defined in the first place?

In fact, attempts like this are nothing but intellectual shortcuts. If there is evidence, or proof, or a valid argument, on either side, then we should examine it. Shortcuts can maybe give us a generic idea where the truth may lie, but they won't give us the truth.

A Lone Straw Man

Another shortcut can be to answer some example of the opponent's view but not completely. This is sometimes called a "Straw Man" argument, and it can happen in a variety of ways. For example, giving a partial picture of the argument, or picking the weakest of your opponent's arguments, and acting like answering that part is the same as disproving the entire viewpoint. The typical whipping-boy on the Theist side is St. Anselm, whose "ontological argument" for God's existence is particularly prone to rejection (even by St. Thomas Aquinas). Kant, Descartes, Hume, and Nietzsche, not to mention practically every member of the New Atheism group, have all had their turn in picking apart, mocking, or answering Anselm's argument, with varying degrees of success (and, for that matter, originality).

I personally think, with Aquinas as well as the other thinkers listed above, that Anselm's argument doesn't work (which is why I won't go to the trouble of explaining it in this book). But disproving an argument for God's existence isn't the same as disproving God. Showing that Anselm's argument doesn't prove God isn't the same as proving there is no God. It just means that this particular way of arriving at a conclusion about God's existence doesn't work. There may very well be other ways that work much better. By the same token, if I'm able to answer, say, Bertrand Russell's arguments against God's existence, that doesn't prove there is a God. It proves that Russell's arguments are inconclusive. I haven't answered "Atheism" as a point of view about the world until I've really dealt with it both fully and honestly; nor has any atheist dealt with "Theism" unless he or she has done the same. In this book, I hope to show at the very least that the Theist argument has not been dealt with fairly by any of the New Atheism authors.

RUSSELL'S TEAPOT AND THE FLYING SPAGHETTI MONSTER: DELICIOUS

Speaking of Bertrand Russell, I suppose it's a good time to mention his famous teapot. Russell argued that believing in God and claiming that this is a reasonable belief because the opposite can't be proven is like believing in a tiny teapot that is circling the earth, too small to be detected by any telescope. "You can't DISprove the existence of God, therefore it is reasonable to believe in him" is like saying "You can't DISprove the existence of a tiny little teapot in Earth's orbit, therefore it is reasonable to believe in one." Later writers changed the image from a teapot, an image admittedly British in its appeal, to something more Continental: the Flying Spaghetti Monster. The argument, of course, runs the same way—you can't PROVE that there isn't an invisible Flying Spaghetti Monster, and so it is quite reasonable to believe in one, if that's a good enough reason to believe in God.

I'm not sure who exactly it was, but at some point Russell must have met a theist who argued that the inability to disprove God makes it reasonable to believe in him. I am not an adherent to this philosophy. I believe the existence of God can be proven, or at the very least given great support through evidence and reasonable argumentation. Perhaps it was the timidity of the theists that Russell had met that gave him the impression of something else.

Of course, Russell was good enough a logician to know that it is practically impossible to prove a Universal Negative proposition (like "there is no God"). Richard Dawkins humbly acknowledges the same: "reason alone could not propel one to total conviction that anything definitely does not exist."[2] But there's another problem here, and it is one of implication. The Flying Spaghetti Monster is thrown around as if the entire Theist argument was nothing but "well you can't DISprove God." Anyone who has done their homework should know that this is simply not the case, and implying otherwise is to muddy up the question, not answer it. It is adding more dust to the air, not clearing it.

---

[2] *The God Delusion*, 74.

An Army of Straw Men

Of course, if answering Anselm isn't enough, answering a whole pile of bad arguments isn't much better. Dawkins (again to take the most popular example) devotes as much time to "the argument from personal experience," "the argument from Scripture," and "the argument from admired religious scientists" as he does to Aquinas's Five Ways, while others (like Christopher Hitchens) attack almost exclusively arguments based on morality, meaning in life, or, worst of all, miracles (which I don't think are meant to be proofs at all, assuming they exist). This isn't to say that these arguments are entirely worthless (though some are); but answering this portion of the Theistic viewpoint doesn't answer the whole question. It doesn't really answer the question at all. In the end, it's nothing but a dodge.

I've got to admit that this isn't any atheist's fault. Theists are themselves so varied in their viewpoints and arguments that I honestly can't blame anyone for having trouble sifting through them all. Of course, this applies as well to atheists: since writing the last chapter, the number of books defending Atheism on my desk has more than doubled (I currently count twenty-five), and I can testify that there's plenty of sifting to do. On the other hand, I think it's dishonest to sift for the dust and not the gold, and there are some arguments for God that are gold, as much dust as there is out there. Similarly, it would have been much easier for me to only quote Dawkins and Hitchens and Krauss, but it would have been dishonest of me not to dig deeper. I don't think it's unreasonable to have expected the same of them.

You Guys Are Jerks

Another major bit of dust that can obscure the eyes is the manner of life of the people adhering to each viewpoint. Theists have committed awful atrocities throughout history; atheists have done the same. Similarly, individuals of both groups have done beautiful things for the whole human race. But neither of these facts proves anything. "The Mormons next door are the nicest people I've met; therefore their religion is the right one" doesn't follow any more than "the atheist boy down the street ran a red light; therefore atheism is wrong."

Despite Hitchens's claim that the atrocities committed by religious people have been *because of* their religion (a claim I will deal with in a later chapter), I don't think establishing a causality is so easy. It would be just as easy to establish that atrocities committed by some Nazi scientists were "because" of science, which I believe is entirely false. But even if establishing causality were easy, it wouldn't prove anything. All theists could be monsters and all atheists angels, and there could still be a God; similarly, all atheists could be monsters and all theists angels, and there could still be no God. You could take it even further: all theists could be monsters *because of* their theism, and all atheists angels *because of* their atheism, and there could still be a God, and vice-versa. The logic simply isn't there to connect these actions to any conclusion about the truth of God's existence, and any side flaunting the moral flaws of the other side isn't doing anything but increasing the dust in the air.

PHILOSOPHY-BASHING: INTELLECTUAL SUICIDE

I'll end this chapter by warning you about one last fallacy (though there are plenty more out there). There's a trend among some of the more scientific-minded of the New Atheism group to disparage philosophy as confusing and useless. Neil Degrasse Tyson has been quoted a number of times insulting philosophy, and I've noticed Richard Dawkins do the same on his Twitter account. Stephen Hawking says it most bluntly: "Traditionally these are questions for philosophy, but philosophy is dead."[3]

Of course, I'd be the first to admit that there are plenty of philosophies that are confusing and useless, but this is a terrible case of throwing the baby out with the bath water. Philosophy, in itself, is nothing more or less than careful, systematic thought. Science is the same, with the added benefits of experimental procedure and mathematical language. This gives philosophy and science both strengths and limitations, and in any case pitting the two against each other as enemies has no basis in either philosophy or science. Dismissing an argument because it is "philosophical" is like dismissing it because it is "thoughtful." It's bad thinking and nothing more. I'll quote perhaps the most thoughtful of the New Atheists here, Daniel Dennett (a philosopher by trade), who makes the point nicely:

> Scientists sometimes deceive themselves into thinking that philosophical ideas are only, at best, decorations or parasitic commentaries on the hard, objective triumphs of science, and that they themselves are immune to the confusions that philoso-

---

[3] Stephen Hawking and Leonard Mlodinow, *The Grand Design* (New York: Bantam Books, 2010), 5.

phers devote their lives to dissolving. But there is no such thing as philosophy-free science; there is only science whose philosophical baggage is taken on board without examination.[4]

DOUBT THYSELF

I challenge you to ask yourself whether you've ever been taken in by any of these fallacies. If so, you owe it to yourself to question whether the foundations of your beliefs are as strong as you think.

---

[4] Daniel C. Dennett, *Darwin's Dangerous Idea: Evolution and the Meaning of Life* (New York: Simon & Schuster, 1995), 21.

CHAPTER THREE

Proof

This Is Gonna Be Hard

There are many thinkers who have attempted to prove that God exists, from Aristotle to Newton. In this chapter, I am presenting the arguments of Thomas Aquinas. I do this not because they are the only ones worth presenting, but because I think they are the clearest. This does not, of course, make them easy to understand. On the contrary, because they are difficult, they are often dismissed. I've even noticed a tendency to just brush aside Thomas's proofs as if they have been fatally disproven. Of course, *saying* a proof doesn't work or has been disproven isn't the same as disproving it; every time I've looked at the actual reasons someone has dismissed these proofs, I've come up empty-handed. I hope to show the emptiness of these objections as well in this chapter.

The point here is that while the difficulty of the proofs is what allows them to be misunderstood, it cannot be any other way. The question itself is a difficult one. Thus an undercurrent throughout this chapter (and perhaps throughout all of our thought about God) is that thinking about God, even the most basic question of whether or not God exists, is challenging in the highest degree, though not impossible. Our minds are up to the task, but we have to use them to the best of our ability. But if you find this chapter too abstract at first, skip it and come back later.

OBJECTIONS: JUST THESE TWO

This difficulty isn't only because the question of God is highly abstract, and it isn't only because of the "dust" kicked up by thinkers on every side. It's difficult because there are real questions to answer—real objections. Aquinas, I think rightly, boils them down to two:

> Objection 1. It seems that God does not exist; because if one of two contraries be infinite, the other would be altogether destroyed. But the word "God" means that He is infinite goodness. If, therefore, God existed, there would be no evil discoverable; but there is evil in the world. Therefore God does not exist.

> Objection 2. Further, it is superfluous to suppose that what can be accounted for by a few principles has been produced by many. But it seems that everything we see in the world can be accounted for by other principles, supposing God did not exist. For all natural things can be reduced to one principle which is nature; and all voluntary things can be reduced to one principle which is human reason, or will. Therefore there is no need to suppose God's existence. (*Summa Theologica* I q. 2, a. 3)[1]

---

[1] All of the quotes from the *Summa* in this chapter are from Book I, question 2, article 3, where Aquinas lays out his "Five Proofs." Thomas

In sum, the two objections to God's existence are:

1. Evil exists in the world, and this cannot harmo-
nize with a good God.

2. The world can be explained without God.

I will deal with the objection of evil in chapter six, while
the second objection will be dealt with as we go through
the Five Ways (Aquinas's five proofs for God's existence),
and more specifically in the next two chapters.

WHAT ARE WE TALKING ABOUT?

Before I look at the First Proof, the proof from motion, I
need to make two notes. First, it might be said that I'm
trying to prove something that I haven't yet defined. What
exactly do I mean by "God?" Dawkins comes up with a decently ecumenical definition that he uses throughout *The
God Delusion*: "a superhuman, supernatural intelligence
who deliberately designed and created the universe and
everything in it, including us."[2]

While I don't think this is a bad definition for the sake
of argument, I won't try defining God at the beginning,
precisely because I haven't presented the proofs yet. While
clarifying terms is important in philosophical debates, as
I noted earlier, it's backwards to begin with a definition
or an idea and then go figure out the arguments that will

Aquinas, *Quaestiones Disputatae De Potentia Dei*, trans. by the English
Dominican Fathers (Westminster, Maryland: The Newman Press, 1952,
reprint of 1932), hereafter abbreviated as *ST*.

2 Dawkins, *The God Delusion*, 52.

prove your point. Perhaps a better way to describe what we're doing is that these arguments *discover* God, and once discovered he can *then* be described. So rather than start out with some definition or another, I will follow Aquinas in allowing the reasoning of the proofs themselves to give me an understanding of what I mean when I say "God." Since there are five of them in this chapter, we will have five angles by which we can describe what this reality is, and perhaps a few more in later chapters.

My second note is a warning. Aquinas is a philosopher of the thirteenth century AD, using terminology coined by Aristotle, a philosopher of the fourth century BC. This unfortunately adds another layer of difficulty to an already difficult question. Much of his terminology isn't familiar to us (like the term "actuality"), and even those terms that would seem familiar (like "motion") are understood in a dramatically different way than we're used to. And yet, despite this, I think Thomas's proofs are still worth hashing through, and, despite an old-fashioned vocabulary (perhaps even an old-fashioned physics), they are still valid and true. We just have to make the effort to understand them.

THE ARGUMENT FROM MOTION: HARD

Thomas begins: "The first and more manifest way is the argument from motion. It is certain, and evident to our senses, that in the world some things are in motion."

That the argument from motion would be the "most manifest way" might be tough to accept if we allow ourselves to get confused by the Aristotelian terminology that follows, but what he means by "manifest" here isn't that this is the easiest proof (or that any of the proofs are easy), but that it begins with the facts most observable to our senses: things change ("motion" means practically any kind of change for Aquinas). This is the bare fact that Thomas uses to build his argument, and the fact that it is something so basic shows us how fundamental he considers God's existence to be. Throughout these proofs, in fact, even a believer might find himself challenged in his or her view of God—this is not a distant God who shoves a miracle through the cracks once in a while when prayers are shouted loudly enough; this is a God who is at the root of every movement and change in the universe.

In any case, no argument has been made yet. He has only presented one premise: things change. Upon this observation (that I don't think anyone can deny) he builds his argument, and this is where it gets hard:

> Now whatever is in motion is put in motion by another, for nothing can be in motion except it is in potentiality to that towards which it is in motion; whereas a thing moves inasmuch as it is in act. For motion is nothing else than the reduction of something from potentiality to actuality.

Don't let the terms distract you. Potentiality just means "it could be but isn't yet" and actuality means "it is right now." So a thing can only move or change when it is able to, and hasn't yet. If my hand is on the desk, it is in potentiality to be raised. Again, I don't see how anyone can disagree with this. But it implies something more. It implies that if something moves or changes, it must by that very fact be part of a chain of movers—that there must be something "before" it that moves it. As far as I can tell, this is a scientific fact, and Lawrence Krauss, one of the New Atheists, says it nicely himself: "Think about it this way. If you are at rest with respect to some charged particle, and you observe it to move, you know it must have experienced a force, because things do not suddenly start moving without a force having acted on them."[3]

Thomas continues:

> But nothing can be reduced from potentiality to actuality, except by something in a state of actuality. Thus that which is actually hot, as fire, makes wood, which is potentially hot, to be actually hot, and thereby moves and changes it. Now it is not possible that the same thing should be at once in actuality and potentiality in the same respect, but only in different respects. For what is actually hot cannot simultaneously be potentially hot; but it is simultaneously potentially cold. It is therefore impossible that in the same respect and in the same way a thing should be both mover and moved, i.e. that it should move itself. Therefore, whatever is in motion must be put in motion by another.

Thomas's example is helpful: wood doesn't spontaneously burst into flame. If that change is to occur, there must be potentiality (the wood "could burn but isn't yet"), but this potentiality can't make itself actual without something acting upon it—the wood can't burn until something moves it to burn, whether this be fire, sunlight, or a spark. Incidentally, if you're wondering about whether, for example, an animal can "move itself" by walking, Aristotle (and Aquinas following him) would answer that one part

---

[3] Lawrence Krauss, "Chapter 4: The Fourth Dimension" in *Hiding in the Mirror: The Mysterious Allure of Extra Dimensions, from Plato to String Theory and Beyond* (New York: Viking, 2005).

moves another (one leg moves another), but no part ever moves itself.

After making this point, Thomas simply applies this principle consistently:

> If that by which it is put in motion be itself put in motion, then this also must needs be put in motion by another, and that by another again.

In other words, if this is the case for the wood lighting on fire, it is the case with all the other changes that led up to that one. There are two ways to imagine this. The first is to rank these moving things as coming before one another *in time*: the wood was ignited by the lighter, which had been previously picked up by the camper, who had been told to start a campfire by his wife, who had been asked to make s'mores by her children, and so on. This isn't exactly what Aquinas has in mind, though in the next chapter we will find that it also ends with the same result.

Aquinas isn't talking about one mover coming after another in time, but *in nature*. That is, one thing is moving another, which is moving another, *all at once*. This is the part that's harder to imagine. The wood is ignited by the lighter, which is *at that moment* held by the camper's hand, which at that moment is being moved by the camper's arm, which is controlled by his nervous system, which is moved (at least in one sense; I'm not going to discuss free will in this book) by the firing of synapses in his brain, which are . . . well, Thomas makes a long story short: **"But this cannot go on to infinity . . . "**

> . . . because then there would be no first mover, and, consequently, no other mover; seeing that subsequent movers move only inasmuch as they are put

in motion by the first mover; as the staff moves only because it is put in motion by the hand.

The reasoning is difficult but airtight: if the chain of movers goes "back" limitlessly (remember, not in time, but *at this moment*), then there is no first one. That is simply the definition of "limitlessly," and Thomas takes this as a possibility for a moment, until he shows just how impossible it is. If it does go on limitlessly, if there is no first, then (by the most basic possible logic) there is no second, no third, no hundredth, and therefore, the fire never ignites. But the fact is, the fire does ignite, as our senses testify.

This part of the argument, that an infinite series of movers is impossible, is commonly misunderstood by those attempting to refute this proof and similar ones that use the same premise. While in earlier works (like the *Summa Contra Gentiles*), Aquinas relies on Aristotle's proofs that an actual infinity is impossible, here he uses the very definition of infinite as "without limit." He simply restates this definition and says this simply means "no first." Then he applies the concept: if there's no first, there's no second either, and so on. You could call this an *a priori* argument, one that relies simply on the concepts themselves to support itself. If "infinite" doesn't mean "no first" then it means nothing at all and is therefore impossible even to think about; if it *does* mean "no first," then the rest of Aquinas's argument follows.

I should note that this argument only works with things that actually exist. There's nothing stopping an infinite series from "existing" in mathematics, or in the past. But we aren't talking about a mathematical abstraction, or about a beginning in time (in fact, Aquinas didn't think you could prove a beginning in time at all). We are talking about here and now, and nothing else. Michael Martin, one of the few atheist thinkers that takes the time to deal with this premise, misses this point: "One wonders why, if there can be infinite sequences in mathematics, there could not be one in causality";[4] the answer, as I implied above, is that mathematical objects only exist in the mind, and we are talking now about reality.

Let me see if I can lay this out a little more clearly so we can get a bird's eye view of the whole argument:

Premise 1: Nothing that changes, changes itself.
Evidence of Premise 1: Observation of all of nature illustrates this.

Premise 2: This cannot go on to infinity.
Evidence of Premise 2: The very definition of "infinity" means "no first," which implies "no second" and therefore "not this change either." But this change has obviously happened.

Conclusion: There must be something that moves other things without itself moving/changes other things without itself changing.

It might be abstract or difficult to think of things on this scale, but no step in the logic is flawed, and no part of the proof is disconnected from reality or from basic reasoning. Numbers, like "first" and "second," are among the clearest possible concepts to the human mind. Motion is the most undoubtable observation we can make. That's all that is needed for this proof to work. In order to escape it, one must deny either the validity of the senses or of

---

4 Michael Martin, *Atheism: A Philosophical Justification* (Philadelphia: Temple University Press, 1990), 97.

the mind. Of course, Descartes is famous for doubting the former, but I don't think materialism (or even science itself) would last very long if it denied the input of the senses (or, what is related to this premise, Newton's laws of motion). As for the latter, a real skeptic might object that human reason and language are limited and cannot know things on such a cosmic scale with such certainty. Ideas like "infinite" and "the whole universe" are too much for us, and the validity of our arguments breaks down when it comes to them. In response to this I ask, where exactly does human reason break down and fail to work, and where is the evidence for that? Why are reason and language reliable when it comes to other things, but not here? This is also not to mention the fact that, in order for the proof to work, we don't need a complete understanding or a clear mental picture of an actual infinity or of the whole universe. We only need to understand that infinite means "without limit" and the whole universe means "all stuff." While some of our basic concepts often are challenged by the develop-ments in our thought (like "space" was challenged by Ein-stein), there is nothing in these basic definitions of infinity or the universe that has been (or perhaps even could be) challenged in any way.

Thomas's argument for the impossibility of an actually infinite chain of movers is one thing, though I wonder if our knowledge of the world today can aid us in understanding this. Let's go back to the example of the camper starting the fire. I stopped with the synapses of his brain firing. These movements would in turn be caused by electrons, which in turn might be said to be moved (in some way) by the forces of nature, for example the force of electromagnetism.

This is where we are taught to stop our thought process, but there is no logical reason to do so. Asking the next question is just as reasonable as asking all the previous ones: What is it exactly that causes the forces of nature to do what they do? It could be argued that the forces of nature are functions of matter and energy (in any case, they're always at the same place at the same time, and it doesn't make much difference for the structure of the argument either way). And why can't we ask what it is that makes matter and energy do what *they* do? Do we go back to the forces of nature, and get ourselves stuck in a circular explanation? (Matter and energy do what they do because of the forces of nature, which do what they do because of matter and energy.) Or do we move another step, and say, for example, that matter and energy do what they do because they are in fact a function of space itself? Then what is it that makes space do what it does? If it changes (for example, if it is expanding, or being filled or emptied of some particle), then according to the same principle we've accepted all along, it can't change itself, but must be changed by something else. Remember: everything that moves is moved by another; the log didn't spontaneously burst into flame. This is something many people seem to forget at this point in the argument.

Many thinkers would begin their evasive maneuvers here. Some, when asked why the universe, all of space-time itself, does what it does, suddenly say "I don't know and we can't know." Others imply that "Science will find out, just wait, but for sure it isn't God." Even worse, some claim, as Krauss does, that it isn't an interesting question: "Either way, what is really useful is not pondering this question, but rather participating in the exciting voyage of discovery that may reveal specifically how the universe in which we live evolved and is evolving and the processes that ultimately operationally govern our existence."[5] He says this

---

[5] Krauss, *A Universe from Nothing*, 178.

about the question "Why is there something rather than nothing?" but it applies just as well here. And the fact is, this isn't an answer to the question. It is a refusal to ask it. It isn't science, and it isn't philosophy. It isn't really thought at all, but only the lack of thought.

If we are serious enough about the truth to attempt to answer the question, we are stuck with Thomas's inescapable reasoning. The chain of movers cannot go back to infinity. There must be a conclusion. But the conclusion to all this is much more modest than people make it out to be:

> Therefore it is necessary to arrive at a first mover, put in motion by no other; and this everyone understands to be God.

Let me again clarify what Aquinas is NOT saying. He is not saying: "Some things move; they are moved by others; this cannot go on to infinity; therefore Baby Jesus will hear your prayers and heal your grandmother." Nor is he taking the same argument and concluding: "therefore marijuana should be illegal." In fact, this argument doesn't even prove (explicitly) that God is immaterial, immortal, all-powerful, that there is one of him, that he moves with a purpose, or that his first name is "God." It proves that there must be something that moves without being moved by anything else; something that causes change without being changed. That's it. What this might later imply is another matter. The proof stops here. But it is a proof, and it does prove what it sets out to prove. All of those other questions are, like I said before, other questions, and Aquinas deals with them separately. Even the last phrase Thomas appends to his proof is a matter of assigning a stipulative definition, as if to say: "if anyone means anything by God, it must mean at least this; let's see where this goes."

Notice, first and foremost, that there is nothing yet miraculous or even personal about the God of this proof. This is a God whose primary work (so far, at least) is in causing the ordinary, day-to-day and moment-to-moment motion we observe in nature—all of it, since everything we said applies to every event we could possibly observe. This is a God who is needed because, if we actually ask the question and answer it honestly, we cannot escape the conclusion that nature does not and cannot explain its own motion by itself. This is a God that works through nature and not against or above it, who acts by means of it, as a musician works by means of his instruments. This is the kind of God that we will get to know in these proofs, and there's a lot more to know. But the first thing we notice when we introduce ourselves to him is that he is ultimately responsible for every motion and change around us, but himself does not and cannot change.

This also implies that the consistency of natural laws and their ability to explain practically everything we observe does not in any way undermine a belief in God as first cause. Quite the contrary, the more consistent and certain, the more inescapable and true the forces and laws of nature are, the more certain we are that God is working. One of the New Atheism thinkers, Victor Stenger, insists on loading the dice against this God, seeking instead a God of pure, supernatural miracles and nothing more:

> My analysis will be based on the contention that God should be detectable by scientific means simply by virtue of the fact that he is supposed to play such a central role in the operation of the universe and the lives of humans. Existing scientific models contain no place where God is included as an ingredient in order to describe observations.

Thus, if God exists, he must appear somewhere within the gaps or errors of scientific models.[6]

The God of the First Way is not one of "gaps or errors;" he is not seeking to cling to some unknown or unknowable corner of the universe, some crack in the quantum flux of things, in order to do what he does. This is a God that works, primarily, through nature itself. The fewer gaps there are in nature, the better we know this God is doing his job. Again, Stenger seems to be seeking something quite different: "We have seen that the origin and the operation of the universe do not require any violations of laws of physics." There is no reason to expect any violation of the laws of physics, and to seek one out as a requirement for believing in God is to misunderstand the entire argument. Even those who believe in miracles wouldn't expect their miraculous God to submit himself to microscopic testing in order to disprove the skepticism of Victor Stenger when this God is already constantly at work in every moment and every event in the universe.

Of course, from this discovery of an Unmoved Mover a few other things can be immediately deduced. If God cannot change, then he has no "potentiality" but is pure Actuality; he is everything he could ever be and could never become anything else, or do anything other than what he does. If he can't move, then he can't be made of parts, which implies also that he is immaterial. These (and many more) are all possible deductions from this first "way," and each of them finds a place in Thomas's later (quite rigorous) development of these ideas. But the proof itself has a single purpose—to show God's existence. In doing so,

---

6 Victor J. Stenger, *God: The Failed Hypothesis: How Science Shows That God Does Not Exist* (Amherst, NY: Prometheus Books, 2008), 13.

however, it has also given us an insight into what God is. In this First Proof, we have learned that God is unchanging and unchangeable, unmoving and immovable, that he is pure Actuality and is not potentially anything else. Each of the five ways will give us its own distinct insight, and that is the real value of working through each one, though I won't spend as much time on the others as I did on this one because they (mostly) follow the same pattern.

Responses to the First Way: "I Don't Get It."

Before I continue with the second of Thomas's proofs, it's worth taking a look at how an atheist might respond to this first one. I have to admit something personal at this point. There have been many times in my life when my belief in God was strengthened and I became more and more confident that it was true that he existed, but nothing strengthened my belief in God as much as reading the books of the New Atheists. This might sound exaggerated or funny of me to say, but I mean it with dead honesty. When I saw for myself how deeply they misunderstood, for example, Aquinas's proofs for God's existence, or how weak their counter arguments were, any remaining doubt I may have had was destroyed.

Let's take the most famous case first. Richard Dawkins summarizes the first three of Thomas's proofs in this way (I haven't found a single atheist writer who actually quotes Aquinas):

1. *The Unmoved Mover.* Nothing moves without a prior mover. This leads us to a regress, from which the only escape is God. Something had to make the first move, and that something we call God.

2. *The Uncaused Cause.* Nothing is caused by itself. Every effect has a prior cause, and again we are pushed back into regress. This has to be terminated by a first cause, which we call God.

3. *The Cosmological Argument.* There must have been a time when no physical things existed. But, since physical things exist now, there must have been something non-physical to bring them into existence, and that something we call God.

All three of these arguments rely upon the idea of a regress and invoke God to terminate it. They make the entirely unwarranted assumption that God himself is immune to regress. Even if we allow the dubious luxury of arbitrarily conjuring up a terminator to an infinite regress and giving it a name, simply because we need one, there is absolutely no reason to endow that terminator with any of the properties normally ascribed to God: omnipotence, omniscience, goodness, creativity of design, to say nothing of such human attributes as listening to prayers, forgiving sins and reading innermost thoughts.[7]

I'd like to point out a couple things here. First, it is a total falsehood that the proofs "invoke God" to terminate an infinite regress. There is no "invocation" involved at all. This is not a "dubious luxury," and it isn't an "arbitrary conjuring." There is only a conclusion that there must be, at some point, something uncaused. This is the end of a logical train of thought that inescapably terminates with this conclusion.

---

[7] Dawkins, *The God Delusion*, 100–101.

Nothing more and nothing less. I've already dealt with the end of this quote from Dawkins, regarding the other "properties" of God, from omnipotence to forgiving sins. Those are simply different questions, and it is bad reasoning to expect this proof to answer every question at once.

The real indicator, however, that Dawkins completely misunderstands this proof is in the sentence: "They make the entirely unwarranted assumption that God himself is immune to regress." The whole conclusion of the proof is that there is a Mover that is Unmoved; that there must be some stopping-point. Dawkins has given no argument or evidence that any point in Aquinas's reasoning is incorrect; he simply disagrees with the conclusion while ignoring the whole proof. Of course, he isn't the first or the only one to do so. Bertrand Russell tells the story of how he discovered this fallacy when he was reading John Stuart Mill:

> I may say that when I was a young man and was debating these questions very seriously in my mind, I for a long time accepted the argument of the First Cause, until one day, at the age of eighteen, I read John Stuart Mill's Autobiography, and there I found this sentence: "My father taught me that the question 'Who made me?' cannot be answered, since it immediately suggests the further question 'Who made God?'" That very simple sentence showed me, as I still think, the fallacy in the argument of the First Cause. If everything must have a cause, then God must have a cause. If there can be anything without a cause, it may just as well be the world as God, so that there cannot be any validity in that argument. It is exactly of the same nature as the Hindu's view, that the world rested upon an elephant and the elephant rested

upon a tortoise; and when they said, "How about the tortoise?" the Indian said, "Suppose we change the subject." The argument is really no better than that. There is no reason why the world could not have come into being without a cause; nor, on the other hand, is there any reason why it should not have always existed. There is no reason to suppose that the world had a beginning at all. The idea that things must have a beginning is really due to the poverty of our imagination. Therefore, perhaps, I need not waste any more time upon the argument about the First Cause.[8]

Russell, who as a philosopher should have known better, makes at least three serious blunders in this single paragraph. The first is the one we saw Dawkins make—asking "who made God?" and revealing that he has no idea what the proof actually says. More fundamental than this is Russell's statement, "If everything must have a cause, then God must have a cause." But "everything must have a cause" is not a premise of the proof, and it is not anything that Aquinas would have claimed. What Aquinas says is not that "everything must have a cause," but that everything *that moves* must be moved; everything *that changes* must be changed. Thirdly, Russell again shows how little he has thought about this proof when he says, "If there can be anything without a cause, it may just as well be the world as God." Thomas showed that *things that move* cannot move themselves—remember the impossibility of the wood igniting without anything acting on it. It doesn't take a lot of observation to realize that the world is changing all the time—in fact, even space-time is, by every account, rapidly

---

[8] Russell, "The First-cause Argument" in *Why I Am Not a Christian*, 6–7.

expanding. So no, the world cannot be the thing "without a cause," if it is itself changing all the time. Russell might disagree with one of Thomas's premises (I don't know how anyone can), but he has given no argument to support himself. He has only shown that he doesn't get it.

Dan Barker makes basically the same mistakes as Bertrand Russell does, and betrays the same ignorance and sloppy philosophy:

> The major premise of this argument, "everything had a cause," is contradicted by the conclusion that "God did not have a cause." You can't have it both ways. If *everything* had to have a cause, then there could not be a first cause. If it is possible to think of a god as uncaused, then it is possible to think the same of the universe.
>
> Some theists, observing that all "effects" need a cause, assert that God is a cause but not an effect. But no one has ever observed an uncaused cause and simply inventing one merely assumes what the argument wishes to prove. If a god can be thought eternal, then so can the universe.[9]

Again, the argument does not state that "everything had a cause;" it is impossible for the universe to be thought of as uncaused because it changes; and someone concluding that there is an uncaused cause (this is, strictly speaking, the Second Proof) is *not* "simply inventing one." It is following reason to its natural conclusion.

Another example of an atheist making the same blunders:

---

[9] Dan Barker, *Godless: How an Evangelical Preacher Became One of America's Leading Atheists* (Berkeley, CA: Ulysses Press, 2008), 114.

If everything has a cause, then God does, too, and there is no first cause. And if something doesn't have a cause, it might as well be the physical world as God or a tortoise.

Of someone who asserts that God is the uncaused first cause (and then preens as if he's really explained something), we should thus inquire, "Why cannot the physical world itself be taken to be the uncaused first cause?" After all, the venerable principle of Occam's razor advises us to "shave off" unnecessary assumptions, and taking the world itself as the uncaused first cause has the great virtue of not introducing the unnecessary hypothesis of God.[10]

And another:

If God created the universe, what created God? To say that God, by definition, is uncreated simply begs the question.[11]

And another:

Nevertheless, the declaration of a First Cause still leaves open the question, "Who created the creator?" After all, what is the difference between arguing in favor of an eternally existing creator versus an eternally existing universe without one?[12]

---

[10] John Allen Paulos, *Irreligion: A Mathematician Explains Why the Arguments for God Just Don't Add Up* (New York: Hill and Wang, 2008), 4–5.

[11] Sam Harris, *Letter to a Christian Nation* (New York: Vintage Books, 2008), 73.

[12] Lawrence Krauss, *A Universe from Nothing*, xxii.

And another:

> If God created and designed all these wonderful
> things, who created God? Supergod? And who
> created Supergod? Superdupergod? Or did God
> create Himself? Was it hard work? Did it take time?
> Don't ask![13]

And another:

> A first cause need not have the properties usually
> associated with God. For example, a first cause
> need not have great, let alone infinite, knowledge
> or goodness.[14]

And another:

> But, if believers are right and "everything" requires
> a cause, then that means something or someone
> must have "caused" their gods as well. They can't
> have it both ways. If, however, they say that there
> is an exception to the rule and their gods can exist
> without anything having caused them, then so can
> the universe.[15]

And another, who doesn't quite understand that this argument isn't about one thing coming before another in time:

> One popular version of the cosmological argu-
> ment can be expressed as follows: the state of the

---

[13] Dennett, *Darwin's Dangerous Idea*, 71.

[14] Michael Martin, *Atheism: A Philosophical Justification*, 97.

[15] Guy P. Harrison, *50 Reasons People Give for Believing in a God* (Amherst, NY: Prometheus Books, 2008), 75.

universe as we see it now was caused by the state of the universe as it was a moment ago; and how it was a moment ago was caused by how it was two moments ago. And how it was two moments ago was caused by how it was three moments ago; and so on. But (so the argument goes) this regress cannot go on infinitely. Therefore there must have been a first cause, and this first cause was (as the originator of everything) God.[16]

My point in all of this is to illustrate that those who reject Thomas's proofs do so based on a clear misunderstanding of them, and not based on any actual refutation of any of his reasoning. It's not just that the proof works—that it proves there is an Unmoved Mover. It's that anyone who claims to reject the proof always gets it wrong, every single time, without exception. I've looked quite earnestly for someone who attempts to give Aquinas a real refutation based on what he is really saying, and have found nothing. Let me know if you have better luck than I do. Honestly.

Dawkins describes, in the first chapter of *The God Delusion*, what he calls the "Einsteinian God." He concludes that Einstein was either a Deist or Pantheist (and leans more toward the latter), but the point is that Einstein certainly did not believe in a "personal God." Rather, Einstein's God was either whatever it is that makes the laws of nature act the way they do, or simply the laws themselves. Even Richard Dawkins is willing to admit that this type of God is worthy of belief. Criticizing a fellow scientist for his religious sycophancy, Dawkins says: "Dyson could easily refute the implication of these quotations from his

---

[16] Nicholas Everitt, *The Non-existence of God* (New York: Routledge, 2004), 60.

Templeton acceptance speech, if only he would explain clearly what evidence he finds to believe in God, in something more than just the Einsteinian sense which, as I explained in Chapter 1, we can all trivially subscribe to."[17] It is interesting to realize that the God of Einstein and even Dawkins (assuming this God is the cause of the laws of nature) is basically the same as the God of Aquinas's First Proof. But the story doesn't stop here.

THE ARGUMENT FROM CAUSALITY: ALSO HARD

Thomas's Second Proof is very similar to the first—in fact, I've spent a lot of time arguing with myself and others about whether it isn't really just the same proof again (Dawkins thinks so, though I think I've shown he's the last person to ask). It seems pretty clear that Aquinas thinks it's different than the First Proof, so let's take a look at it:

> The second way is from the nature of the efficient cause. In the world of sense we find there is an order of efficient causes. There is no case known (neither is it, indeed, possible) in which a thing is found to be the efficient cause of itself; for so it would be prior to itself, which is impossible. Now in efficient causes it is not possible to go on to infinity, because in all efficient causes following in order, the first is the cause of the intermediate cause, and the intermediate is the cause of the ultimate cause, whether the intermediate cause be several, or only one. Now to take away the cause is to take away the effect. Therefore, if there be no

---

[17] Dawkins, *The God Delusion*, 183.

first cause among efficient causes, there will be no
ultimate, nor any intermediate cause. But if in efficient causes it is possible to go on to infinity, there
will be no first efficient cause, neither will there be
an ultimate effect, nor any intermediate efficient
causes; all of which is plainly false. Therefore it is
necessary to admit a first efficient cause, to which
everyone gives the name of God.

If the structure seems familiar, that's because it is: begin
with an observable fact, and reason from there—again,
being cornered by the impossibility of an infinite trail back-
ward, some "first" must be posited if anything is to make
any sense. In this case, the observable fact isn't change, but
being itself (this is what sets it apart from the First Proof).

"Efficient cause" can be applied to many things, since
it simply means "agent" or "doer." It's simply something
that makes something else be a certain way, or be at all.
There can be efficient causes of motion, and we dealt with
those in the First Proof; in this case, we are looking at
efficient causes of existence. It's not that the wood needs
a cause for it to ignite, it's that it needs a cause for it to
exist: nothing is the "efficient cause of itself" because in
that case it would be "prior to itself." Again this can be
taken in both a natural and a temporal sense—and it is
true in both senses. A tree is not "prior to itself" in the
sense of "before itself" in time—that is, it needed to have
come from something else (a previous tree, in this case) at
some time in the past if it is going to exist now. It can't
have caused itself to exist, because in that case it would
exist "before" itself in time.

But again the same argument can be made by taking
"prior" to mean at the same time, but "before" in the order
of causes (remember the hand holding the lighter igniting

the wood, all at once). In this way, the existence of the atmosphere is required *right now* for the existence of the oxygen around earth, which is required for a living ecosystem, which is required for that particular forest, which is required for the existence of that individual tree.

In the same way as with the argument from motion, no element in this elaborate combination of interdependent relationships can be a cause for itself (whether right now or in time), and so the same argument about an infinite regress applies here, resulting in the conclusion that "it is necessary to admit a first efficient cause, to which everyone gives the name of God." It may be the case that at some point this proof and the first one "overlap," since we can perhaps say that there is an atmosphere around earth "because" of the force of gravity, which is the way it is because of the nature of space-time.

Here again we need to ask: is there anything in space-time that implies that it *must* exist? Hume brings this up as a possibility, letting his character Philo speak for him: "But further, why may not the material universe be the necessarily existent Being, according to this pretended explication of necessity? We dare not affirm that we know all the qualities of matter; and, for aught we can determine, it may contain some qualities which, were they known, would make its non-existence appear as great a contradiction as that twice two is five."[18] Certainly the expansion of space-time, and the effect that mass has on it, indicate that it is in a constant state of change, and so it cannot be the Unmoved Mover if it is in motion. But what about here? Can we say that space-time can itself be the First Cause, without need to posit another?

---

[18] David Hume, *Dialogues Concerning Natural Religion*, ed. Richard H. Popkin (Indianapolis: Hackett, 1998), pt. IX.

Space-time possesses nothing to imply that it must exist. In fact, we know from the Big Bang that it didn't exist at all at some point. Lawrence Krauss, again with admirable honesty, admits this: "The apparent logical necessity of First Cause is a real issue for any universe that has a beginning. Therefore, on the basis of logic alone one cannot rule out such a deistic view of nature."[19] But even aside from the Big Bang (which Aquinas didn't know about), the very structure of space-time suggests the complete opposite when we remember the logic of the First Proof and how it applied to motion. If something moves, that is, if it changes, it cannot be first, by definition, since it cannot move itself and therefore must be moved by another. Aquinas, who is perhaps the most concise of writers (don't let the sheer volume of his writings mislead you), expects us to remember this element of the logic of the First Proof, and apply it here.

The distinction between existence and motion, between being and becoming, allows us to come to a second insight into God's nature, derived from this proof: God is not only an Unchanging Changer or Unmoving Mover, but he is a First Cause of being—it's not only everything that *happens* that depends utterly on God, but also everything that *is*.

THE ARGUMENT FROM NECESSITY: EVEN HARDER

The Third Proof is the first that mentions time, and while it contains some terminology that needs explaining, it also is worth our attention:

The third way is taken from possibility and necessity, and runs thus. We find in nature things that are

---

[19] Krauss, *A Universe from Nothing*, 173.

possible to be and not to be, since they are found to be generated, and to corrupt, and consequently, they are possible to be and not to be. But it is impossible for these always to exist, for that which is possible not to be at some time is not. Therefore, if everything is possible not to be, then at one time there could have been nothing in existence. Now if this were true, even now there would be nothing in existence, because that which does not exist only begins to exist by something already existing. Therefore, if at one time nothing was in existence, it would have been impossible for anything to have begun to exist; and thus even now nothing would be in existence—which is absurd. Therefore, not all beings are merely possible, but there must exist something the existence of which is necessary. But every necessary thing either has its necessity caused by another, or not. Now it is impossible to go on to infinity in necessary things which have their necessity caused by another, as has been already proved in regard to efficient causes. Therefore we cannot but postulate the existence of some being having of itself its own necessity, and not receiving it from another, but rather causing in others their necessity. This all men speak of as God.

What "necessity" means, as opposed to "possibility" is clearer in definition than it is in application. Things that are "possible" are simply things that "might not be," and things that are "necessary" are things that "must be." From this distinction, Thomas begins ruling out different scenarios that could have resulted in our universe. Certainly if there is nothing necessary, if everything that exists is only possible, then our universe could not have resulted.

The kinds of things he has in mind here are plants and animals—things that come and go, that begin and end existing.

But he continues, getting to the real point (since I don't think anyone has posited that animals and plants are the ultimate, most basic realities of the universe). Some things, to Thomas, are necessary—they simply must exist in any imaginable world. He would have had in mind things like the stars, which medieval cosmology would have seen as endless and unchanging, as well as the basic elements. We know today that the stars can come and go, just on a radically different time scale than plants and animals. We also know that the matter that makes up the elements isn't as basic as once thought—that it can be broken down into smaller particles, and it can also be converted to energy. But we can translate Thomas's meaning by positing that the things that are "necessary" are the most fundamental particles and forces of nature. Assuming there is a universe, that there is space-time, that there is matter and energy, the basic forces of, for example, gravity and electromagnetism, must be as they are. They have necessity.

This is a debatable claim, of course, and one of the most fascinating discussions happening in science today is whether there could have been (or currently are) universes where the forces of nature are different than they are in our universe. Krauss has this to say:

> In the first place, the question of what determined the laws of nature that allowed our universe to form and evolve now becomes less significant. If the laws of nature are themselves stochastic and random, then there is no prescribed "cause" for our universe. Under the general principle that anything that is not forbidden is allowed, then we would be

guaranteed, in such a picture, that some universe would arise with the laws that we have discovered. No mechanism and no entity is required to fix the laws of nature to be what they are. They could be almost anything. Since we don't currently have a fundamental theory that explains the detailed character of the landscape of a multiverse, we cannot say. (Although to be fair, to make any scientific progress in calculating possibilities, we generally assume that certain properties, like quantum mechanics, permeate all possibilities. I have no idea if this notion can be usefully dispensed with, or at least I don't know of any productive work in this regard.)[20]

Which of the "laws" (it seems to me "forces" is a better word to use here, but I'll save that for the next chapter) are truly necessary, and which can be dispensed with, is a great question that I'd love to know the answer to, but it's not exactly our topic here. Krauss suggests that in any universe in the "multiverse" (again, I'll have more to say about that later), it's hard to imagine realities like quantum mechanics not existing.

Whatever the case, it must be one of two possibilities. Either some of these basic forces are necessary, or none are. If none of them are necessary, then Thomas can skip the part of his proof where he discusses necessary things and go right to his conclusion that God is the being whose necessity is not caused by anything else. But if there are necessary forces that *must* exist, the second part of the argument becomes relevant:

---

[20] Krauss, *A Universe from Nothing*, 176–177.

But every necessary thing either has its necessity caused by another, or not. Now it is impossible to go on to infinity in necessary things which have their necessity caused by another, as has been already proved in regard to efficient causes. Therefore we cannot but postulate the existence of some being having of itself its own necessity, and not receiving it from another, but rather causing in others their necessity. This all men speak of as God.

The question at hand is whether the most necessary, un-changing, basic things in the universe (whatever they might be) simply explain themselves, and cannot be oth-erwise than they are. Bertrand Russell poses the question in this way:

Natural laws are a description of how things do in fact behave, and being a mere description of what they in fact do, you cannot argue that there must be somebody who told them to do that, because even supposing that there were, you are then faced with the question "Why did God issue just those natural laws and no others?"[21]

His question at the end is beside the point—why God does this or that, whether he also is bound by logical or any other kind of necessity, is another question (e.g., "Can God make a rock so heavy he can't lift it?"). What is at hand here is whether the natural forces are absolutely nec-essary, or could be otherwise than they are, or could not have existed at all.

---

[21] Russell, "The Natural-law Argument" in *Why I Am Not a Christian*, 8.

Hume was insightful enough to realize the interdependency between natural forces and the matter and energy they govern. Again speaking through Philo, he asks:

> Is it not probable, I ask, that the whole economy of the universe is conducted by a like necessity, though no human algebra can furnish a key which solves the difficulty? And instead of admiring the order of natural beings, may it not happen that, could we penetrate into the intimate nature of bodies, we should clearly see why it was absolutely impossible they could ever admit of any other disposition?[22]

Natural forces really exist when matter and energy exist, or at the very least when space-time exists. There is no actual gravity where there is no influence of matter with mass, and not even the possibility of a gravitational field where there is no space. The gravitational field is only an idea without actual space for it to function in, and I doubt any materialist would posit a Platonic "world of ideas" that has any independent reality apart from the actual universe.

Thus, the necessity of the natural forces requires and assumes the existence of the universe. This Third Proof builds upon the Second Proof—necessity is a consequence of being. And if being cannot be accounted for apart from a First Cause, neither can necessary beings be accounted for apart from a Necessary Being, one that has his own necessity in himself, and causes any other necessary thing both to be, and to be necessary. The God of the Third Proof is one who explains his own necessary existence—he cannot not be.

---

[22] Hume, *Dialogues Concerning Natural Religion,* pt. IX.

The Argument from Goodness: Eh . . .

The Fourth Proof would seem, to our eyes, to move to another plane of existence entirely. It looks not so much cosmic as local, and not so much universal as human:

> The fourth way is taken from the gradation to be found in things. Among beings there are some more and some less good, true, noble and the like. But "more" and "less" are predicated of different things, according as they resemble in their different ways something which is the maximum, as a thing is said to be hotter according as it more nearly resembles that which is hottest; so that there is something which is truest, something best, something noblest and, consequently, something which is uttermost being; for those things that are greatest in truth are greatest in being, as it is written in Metaph. ii. Now the maximum in any genus is the cause of all in that genus; as fire, which is the maximum heat, is the cause of all hot things. Therefore there must also be something which is to all beings the cause of their being, goodness, and every other perfection; and this we call God.

Remember that Thomas said that the First Proof, that from motion, is the most "manifest" way. That means that the premise it relies upon, the reality of motion or change, is the most obvious to us—indeed, we'd have to deny the very validity of our senses in order to escape it. The Second Proof, from the causality of being, is based on a premise that is clear, but less directly "sensible," since it introduces the concept of existence. The third is even more abstract, adding the idea of necessity. Here we have, on the one hand, a further abstraction, the idea of goodness, but on the other hand, something more accessible to human life.

What Thomas means by "good" here is not at all "moral good," as in "it is good to help people." He means a natural good, as in "ice cream is good." A good, in ancient and medieval philosophy, is simply something desirable for any reason. In that tradition, there was a clear distinction between "real" and "apparent" goods—that is, between things that we should really desire and things that we shouldn't, but seem attractive anyway. Add to this the metaphysical arguments that "those things that are greatest in truth are greatest in being," and "the maximum in any genus is the cause of all in that genus," and you have a pretty complicated mess to work through, by modern standards. Hence this proof might be, in the end, the least accessible to us today.

The proof itself does not have a complicated structure. If there are going to be things in the world that are good, and other things that are better, then there must be some best thing. This sounds weak to our ears because our culture understands good and better in subjective terms— good *for me* or better *for you*. This isn't to say that there is no objective good—something that we all truly desire, and that is truly desirable. As far as our culture has come from Thomas's worldview, most of us can agree that, for example, knowledge is better than ignorance—truly better, and not just a personal preference. We might not agree on whether thin crust pizza is better than thick crust (it is), but most of us would agree that life is better than death. If this comparison is real, and if life *really* is better than death, the logical question would be "better in reference to what?" Certainly the human being is one real reference point, but that runs the risk of making even these most basic "goods" become utterly subjective, because there might be some human being out there who thinks that death is better than life, or that ignorance is better than knowledge (and I'm sure there are). This Fourth Proof sees the need for a terminus, an end-point, in good things—a "Best"—that which is most desirable, and really, truly so. Otherwise, as Aristotle says, "all human desire would be in vain."[23] Interestingly, Aristotle says this in order to show that human happiness must exist, and only later (in *Nicomachean Ethics* Book X and *Metaphysics* XII) ties this act of happiness to the contemplation of God.

Nevertheless, this Fourth Proof, unlike the first three, has a premise that can technically be denied. If we were to say that there is no real good, nothing truly desirable except what we arbitrarily, subjectively want, that there is no purpose or fulfillment or true happiness, that ignorance and knowledge are equally worthless, that life and death are equally empty, then we have no need of a "Best." Not in a world like that, where there is no good. But if you accept that there really is a "good" and "better" out there, "Best" is not far behind. In any case, if one were to accept its premises, this Fourth Proof adds to the previous titles of God that he is that which is most desirable, the greatest Good.

THE ARGUMENT FROM GOVERNANCE: EASY TO SCREW UP

The Fifth Proof, sometimes called the "Argument from Design," is the most popular today. This can often be unfortunate: I've seen some embarrassing versions of this argument, ranging from the "eye of God" in the Helix Nebula

---

[23] Aristotle, *Nicomachean Ethics* I, a. 2.

to the suitability of the banana to the human hand. Please spare yourselves these arguments and go straight to the source (I'd advise this when you do anything—from studying literature to hearing the news). Here is how Aquinas states it:

> The fifth way is taken from the governance of the world. We see that things which lack intelligence, such as natural bodies, act for an end, and this is evident from their acting always, or nearly always, in the same way, so as to obtain the best result. Hence it is plain that not fortuitously, but designedly, do they achieve their end. Now whatever lacks intelligence cannot move towards an end, unless it be directed by some being endowed with knowledge and intelligence; as the arrow is shot to its mark by the archer. Therefore some intelligent being exists by whom all natural things are directed to their end; and this being we call God.

Though there might be a certain accessibility to this proof, I think it's unadvisable to take it in isolation from the first four. On the contrary, I think it requires them and builds on them. Using it on its own, one could present it like this: "See the beauty and complex order of this novel/cell phone/ painting? There's no way it all just randomly fell together like this. All the more so the universe and everything in it. It is too complex to be accounted for by random chance."

Stating it this way is problematic for many reasons, but certainly one of them is that it makes a straw man out of the materialist opponent. No atheist worth his salt would say that all the order of the universe is the result of blind chance. The universe is the way it is because of an intricate combination of natural forces acting on matter and energy in space. Nor is the evocation of some law or another a good answer to this position (I myself get irritated when someone says "Second Law of Thermodynamics" and folds their arms in triumph; I can't imagine what a physicist feels like).

The second reason this oversimplification is problematic is that it tries to prove a God of miracles, not of nature. All along it is the God who created the world who is the object of the proofs—a God who is the reason behind all the forces and laws that govern everything around us. Thus a false dichotomy is created, ironically by the theistic side of the debate, between order that is the result of natural forces and order that is caused by God. All this is the result of taking the Fifth Proof as a stand-alone. Aquinas didn't do this, and he didn't see the argument from order as the best or strongest way. On the contrary, he placed it last because it requires the first four in order to work as a proof at all.

The question at hand is not whether all the order in the world can be accounted for by natural forces. Thomas's position is not to find a flaw in these forces or a "gap" that they don't explain, and then to insert God there. That whole procedure is intellectually dishonest. The way Thomas proceeds (and in this way, and in many others, he is much more contemporary than many who came after him) is to show that the order of the universe is the result of natural forces that are in turn caused by a God who is the ultimate agent in ordering the world. This is not an either/or question— either God orders the universe or the forces of nature do. God orders the universe *by means of* the natural forces he created. Otherwise, why would he create them in the first place?

So the argument assumes the "chains" given in the first three proofs, as well as the "end" (or "good") given in the

Fourth Proof. What this Fifth Proof adds, however, is quite significant. It adds intelligence. God as Mover, as Cause of being, as Necessary being, as Ultimate Good, account for movement, being, necessity, and goodness, respectively. But order is a distinct issue, and it also must be accounted for logically. But just as it isn't enough to explain movement to stop at intermediate movers, it isn't enough to explain order to stop at intermediate orderers. These forces need explanation just like everything else, especially because they are themselves so remarkably ordered (one word for this in physics is "symmetry"). In fact, the forces of nature are so precisely ordered that their action is best expressed in mathematical terms, the most precise language we have. Whence this precision, except from a being capable of being precise? Whence this order, except from a being capable of ordering, that is, a being having intelligence?

I repeat, it doesn't work to show the consistency of natural forces and the vast amount of natural phenomena they explain, and act as if this is somehow an objection to God's existence. Quite the contrary. The more consistent natural forces are, the more God's intelligence is implied, and the more they explain in nature, the more certain it is that God is working. There's an odd debate, at least in America, about evolution as a natural phenomenon being able to explain the intricate development of life, and perhaps even its origin, without the need for a direct miracle from anything apart from natural causes. I will discuss evolution in a later chapter, but I'll blow the ending right now: it would not have been difficult in the least for a medieval scholastic God-fearing philosopher to affirm that life can come from non-living things, simply by the ordinary activity of natural forces.

Let's go back to one of the bad examples I brought

up before, and see if we can make it work. Let's say the novel *A Tale of Two Cities* is a superlative example of what story structure, narrative style, and character development should be (plug in any novel you like if you disagree with my choice). It follows all the "rules" of every part of a novel. If these rules were as precise as some of the laws of physics we have discovered, you could argue (and a materialist most likely would) that these rules dictated everything in the book, down to the last letter. Even if this were the case, the rules of story structure and character development and English prose would not have written the novel; Charles Dickens wrote the novel, and he used these rules in order to do it. The fact that it follows the rules—that the story rises and falls, that the characters struggle and change, and that the sentences flow (sometimes extraordinarily long) according to the strictest possible rules of story structure and English grammar—does not take away at all from the fact that the novel's author is Charles Dickens. Like I said just now, the rules of story, character, and even grammar aren't nearly as precise as those of physics; in fact, I'd argue they aren't even "rules" in the same sense. But the analogy does illustrate the point: laws, rules, forces, do not disprove an original author or designer behind them, but rather confirm one—especially when, in the case of the universe, it is precisely the rules that the Author composed in the first place.

I'll have more to say about the laws of nature in the next chapter, but I'd like to conclude this one by making a few final points. First, if you look back on these arguments and feel a little overwhelmed, or even skeptical that we could go from something as small as lighting a campfire to something as big as God, go back over the arguments and see where exactly your objection lies. The arguments are admittedly difficult, and the subject matter is enormous, but the fact is the logic is there, step-by-step, from beginning to end, without a crack. If you can see every step but the argument doesn't click, it's not the argument that is the problem. Our minds must expand if they are to see it all together, and this expansion is exactly where the exhilaration of philosophy lies. But we must trust our reasoning enough to affirm that if there is no flaw, then the argument works, whether we see it all with a single intuition or not. Few people can understand General Relativity with a single insight—it is the result of a combination of reasons that force us to that conclusion; that doesn't mean that General Relativity is untrue.

I repeat something I've already said many times: We haven't proven the validity of the Bible, or the fact of the Resurrection, or the immortality of the human soul. We haven't explicitly proven that there is one God, or that he is all-powerful. But if these proofs work, then I challenge you to take these other questions just as seriously, and be just as patient with them as you have been with this long-winded ordeal of a chapter.

We have discovered that there is an Unmoved Mover who doesn't change; a First Cause of all that exists; a Necessary Being; one that is all Good and the cause of all goodness; finally, we have discovered that there is an Intelligence behind all the order of our world. Of course, you could reject the Intelligence behind the forces of nature by denying that they are ordered. You'd lose the symmetry which is the basis of science, but at least you'd get rid of God. You could also reject the primal Goodness by throwing away any true meaning in life. You'd have to face that, but at least God wouldn't get in your way. You could reject the Necessary Being, the First Cause and the Unmoved Mover by denying your senses and the validity of your reason to make it that far. You could do any of these things;

but, if you did, I'd be forced to ask whether you're really searching for the truth, or just desperate to deny God's existence.

CHAPTER FOUR

THE BIG BANG

DOES YOUR MOM KNOW YOU'RE STUPID? AN EXCURSUS ON MODES OF CAUSALITY

I remember an elementary school taunt that went something like this: "Does your mom know you're stupid?" The fourth-grader, faced with this intimidating question for the first time and seeing his whole playground reputation at stake, tenses up and quickly, vehemently answers "NO!" After this, the giggles of his classmates begin, the music in the background takes on a sour tone, and the clouds cover the sun as his interlocutor proceeds to the punchline: "Well maybe you should tell her!" Laughter begins to thunder from the swing set to the basketball court as our fourth-grader realizes his folly, and is forced to flee in fury and shame while his classmates point and laugh and rain pours down mercilessly upon his humiliated head.

All childhoods are a bit tragic, but I'm telling this sad story not as social commentary on the state of the educational system today, but to give an example of what, in philosophy, is called a "Complex Question;" that is, a question that contains two or more questions but presents itself as one. Our example above is really a combination of the questions "Are you stupid?" and "Is your mother aware of this fact?" Some complex questions are more complex and thus more difficult to peel apart. "Was the universe created by God or by the Big Bang?" This is a combination of many questions:

- Was the universe created by God?
- Was the universe created by the Big Bang?
- Is it necessarily one or the other or could it have been both?
- If it can't be both, why?
- If it can be both, how?

Another fallacy (the "dust" I talked about in chapter two) that's contained in such questions is named "False Dichotomy" or "False Dilemma"—an implication that it must be only one thing or the other (in this case, God or the Big Bang), when it's possible it could be both. We'll run into this again in the next chapter when we discuss evolution.

Of course, if a thing can be caused by more than one thing, it must be in different ways. A child can be caused by both her father and her mother, but they are both causing in different ways. This sentence was written in one way by my brain, in another way by my fingers, and in another way by my computer. Anyone interested in these different "modes of causality" can take a look at the writings of Aristotle, and they'd have a ball, but I don't need to go into much more detail here.

The word "cause" itself can mean a few different things. It can be the answer to "why?" For example: *Why did you smile? Because I remembered a joke I heard earlier.* Or: *Why did you come here? Because I need to borrow your lawnmower.* In another sense, "cause" can answer the question "how?" *What caused the rain to fall? The accumulation of water particles in a cloud,* or *The force of gravity pulling the drops of water to the earth.*

Scientists are quite ready to make this distinction, of course. I'll quote Lawrence Krauss as a good example:

> Whenever one asks "Why?" in science, one actually means "How?". "Why?" is not really a sensible question in science because it usually implies purpose and, as anyone who has been the parent of a small child knows, one can keep on asking "Why?" forever, no matter what the answer to the previous question. Ultimately, the only way to end the conversation seems to be to say "Because!"[1]

That there is a difference between "why" and "how" is clear enough, though I wonder whether the two questions are as isolated as Krauss makes them seem. The question of "why" is often rejected, as by Krauss above, as unscientific, "teleological," and (worst of all, in some eyes,) "philosophical." Once this rejection of "why" is made, the question of "how" is affirmed to be in the domain only of modern science. I think both of these conclusions are false—"why" is a perfectly valid question, and "how" can have many different aspects.

In this chapter, both questions will be asked, because I think both can lead us to a conclusion about the nature of the universe and of God. If we take the "how" approach, we are led to the question "how was the Big Bang caused?" That is, unless we arbitrarily choose to stop our thought process and not ask that question. If we take the "why" approach, we are led to the question "why is there something rather than nothing?" This question is connected to the Second, Third, and Fourth Proofs discussed in the previous chapter, but I'll leave that to your own consideration.

---

[1] Krauss, *A Universe from Nothing*, xiv.

History: Meddling Scientist Priests

First, a bit of history. Many times I've been surprised to find that atheists posit the Big Bang as a stand-alone proof that there is no Creator, and seem utterly unaware of the fact that it was first proposed by a Catholic priest. Some of the New Atheism books completely neglect to mention this fact (though nobody has the gall to deny it). Victor Stenger, as aggressive as he is against theism, is more forthright than others in his presentation of the Big Bang theory's historical development: "The idea behind a big bang was first proposed in 1927 by astronomer and Belgian Catholic priest George-Henri Lemaître, although he did not use the term *big bang*. He showed that an expanding universe was perfectly consistent with Einstein's general relativity."[2] Stephen Hawking is similarly honest:

> But in 1927 a professor of physics and Roman Catholic priest named Georges Lemaître proposed a similar idea: if you trace the history of the universe backward into the past, it gets tinier and tinier until you come upon a creation event—what we now call the big bang.
>
> Not everyone liked the big bang picture. In fact, the term "big bang" was coined in 1949 by Cambridge astrophysicist Fred Hoyle, who believed in a universe that expanded forever, and meant the term as a derisive description.[3]

---

[2] Stenger, *God and the Folly of Faith: The Incompatibility of Science and Religion* (Amherst, NY: Prometheus Books, 2012), 168.
[3] Hawking and Mlodinow, *The Grand Design*, 127.

Like any scientific theory, the Big Bang was looked at skeptically at first (even by Einstein), until sufficient evidence for it surfaced. But unlike most theories, the Big Bang came with "baggage" that contained a tinge of theistic, if not religious, implication: "Believers were overjoyed when the Big Bang theory was confirmed in a whole series of astronomical observations, starting with the serendipitous discovery of the cosmic background radiation by radio astronomers Arno Penzias and Robert Wilson in 1964."[4] I'll review the atheistic interpretations of the Big Bang later in the chapter, but my point here is that it is really odd for anyone to take the Big Bang as obviously implying that there is no Creator, when historically it was very much the opposite.

A Beginning in Time: Getting Defensive

Aquinas's proofs reviewed in the previous chapter assume that we don't know from reason alone that the world had a beginning (Thomas held the beginning of time as a "revealed" truth from Scripture). That is, as far as Aquinas could tell from his senses, the world had always been around (he gets this, like much of his cosmology, from Aristotle). Thus his proofs, as I hope I made clear, do not rely on a beginning in time in order to be valid. Had he known what we know today, I think he would have had a much easier time proving God's existence.

Imagine someone walking quietly into a room with an alarmed look on his face, closing the door behind him, sitting down rigidly and nervously, and without being asked, stating in a loud, forced tone, "I didn't break the

---

4 Stenger, *God and the Folly of Faith*, 170.

lamp." While this is far from scientific proof that he did, in fact, break the lamp, it should be more than enough to arouse our suspicion.

The very defensiveness with which many atheist writers approach a beginning in time (though a beginning in time isn't something universally agreed upon) reveals a weakness in their own argument. A subtle such defensiveness can be detected in David Hume: "Add to this, that in tracing an eternal succession of objects, it seems absurd to inquire for a general cause or first Author. How can anything, that exists from eternity, have a cause, since that relation implies a priority in time and a beginning of existence?"[5] But Bertrand Russell reveals it a little more clearly: "There is no reason why the world could not have come into being without a cause; nor, on the other hand, is there any reason why it should not have always existed. There is no reason to suppose the world had a beginning at all. The idea that things must have a beginning is really due to the poverty of our imagination."[6] His mistake is to link causality to precedence in time, but even aside from this, his attitude seems to suggest that it would be problematic for the atheistic viewpoint if it were shown that the universe did not always exist.

If this is too subtle, consider the defensiveness of dismissing the entire question. Again, Bertrand Russell (in some ways the no-godfather of the New Atheism movement) is a good illustration of this. In a debate with Fr. Frederick Copleston—a famous philosopher who wrote *A History of Philosophy*, dwarfing Bertrand Russell's in size and, I believe, competency—Russell utterly and explicitly evades the entire question:

---

[5] Hume, *Dialogues Concerning Natural Religion*, pt. IX.
[6] Russell, "The First-Cause Argument" in *Why I Am Not a Christian*, 8.

COPLESTON: Your general point then, Lord Russell, is that it is illegitimate even to ask the question of the cause of the world?

RUSSELL: Yes, that is my position.[7]

This has become, for many in the New Atheism school of thought, a kind of mantra. Of course, saying that the question is "illegitimate" is the equivalent of any other name-calling in an argument.

Nothing

Krauss takes up Russell's flag and runs with it, but with greater scientific precision. The issue is not so much a beginning in time, but the existence of anything at all:

> Why is there something rather than nothing? Ultimately, this question may be no more significant or profound than asking why some flowers are red and some are blue. "Something" may always come from nothing. It may be required, independent of the underlying nature of reality. Or perhaps "something" may not be very special or even very common in the multiverse. Either way, what is really useful is not pondering this question, but rather participating in the exciting voyage of discovery that may reveal specifically how the universe in which we live evolved and is evolving and the processes that ultimately operationally govern our existence.[8]

---

[7] Debate between Bertrand Russell and Frederick Copleston, printed in John Leslie and Robert Lawrence Kuhn, eds., *The Mystery of Existence: Why Is There Anything at All?* (Malden, MA: Wiley-Blackwell, 2013), 55.

[8] Krauss, *A Universe from Nothing*, 178.

That it isn't a "useful" question to ask is, at the very least, in the eye of the beholder; but even more, I'd like to ask Krauss why the question isn't an important part, maybe the most important part, of the "voyage of discovery" he cares so much about. Why is it that only "how" matters? "Not only has 'why' become 'how' but 'why' no longer has any verifiable meaning" (Lawrence Krauss, *A Universe from Nothing*, xv). In fact, I'd push my question even further and ask why it is that even "how" has to stop at specifically the moment that is convenient for the atheistic position?

Just as bad as the name-calling is another false dichotomy between the questions. After explaining that his book will show how empty space is able to produce matter, Krauss continues:

> For many people, however, the fascinating possible resolutions of these age-old mysteries are not sufficient. The deeper question of nonexistence overwhelms them. Can we understand how absolute nothingness, without even the potential for anything at all to exist, does not still reign supreme? Can one ever say anything other than the fact that the nothing that became our something was a part of "something" else, in which the potential for our existence, or any existence, was always implicit?
>
> In the book I take a rather flippant attitude toward this concern, because I don't think it adds anything to the productive discussion, which is "What questions are actually answerable by probing the universe?" I have discounted this philosophical issue, but not because I think those people who occupy themselves with certain aspects of it are not trying hard to define logical questions. Rather, I discount this aspect of philosophy here because I

think it bypasses the really interesting and answerable physical questions associated with the origin and evolution of our universe. No doubt some will view this as my own limitation, and maybe it is. But it is within that context that people should read this book. I don't make any claims to answer any questions that science cannot answer, and I have tried very carefully within the text to define what I mean by "nothing" and "something." If those definitions differ from those you would like to adopt, so be it. Write your own book. But don't discount the remarkable human adventure that is modern science because it doesn't console you.[9]

As always, I appreciate Krauss's honesty in admitting that "science can't answer" the question at hand, which in this case is not the question of "why" but of "how" absolute nothingness can produce anything. This leaves us with the following conclusions, which I think are quite valid: First, that science is able to answer an infinite number of questions with beautiful and astounding precision and experimental certainty, concluding with the question, "How can empty space produce something?" But that's where science stops. The question of "why" anything happens, as we will see, is outside the realm of scientific inquiry. But even more, the critical question in the search for an answer about God's existence is also outside the realm of scientific inquiry: *How* can absolute nothingness produce something?

---

[9] Krauss, *A Universe from Nothing*, xvi–xvii.

SCIENCE = MATH + EXPERIMENT

That "why" is a question for (I'd say) philosophy and (Krauss would say) certainly not science, is easy enough to explain. Science as we have it today is able to do what it does because of the language it speaks, which is the language of mathematics (this was one of Galileo's great contributions to the history of thought). But while mathematics is amazing in its precision in describing how things happen, it cannot even *ask* the question "why," much less answer it. It is simply not the kind of question that it is able to interact with at all. Mathematics gives science its great precision, but also this limitation.

As for the second question, "how" absolute nothingness can produce something, Krauss is quite right in noting this is also a question outside the bounds of science, but for a different reason. The two real pillars of modern science are mathematical expression and experimental procedure. We can experiment on basically anything; we can even experiment on empty space (what Krauss sometimes defines as "nothing"). But we can't experiment on absolute non-being. "Where" there's no space (or time, for that matter), there's no possibility for experiment or observation. That leaves the "how" question completely outside the realm of science, which is why philosophers are so comfortable with it while many scientists (as I hope to show) completely botch it.

I suppose it's worthwhile at this point to answer another implicit question. Someone may posit that the *only* real knowledge is that produced by empirical science, and that everything else is only opinion. I've rarely come across this explicitly stated, though the earliest I can trace the implication is to Francis Bacon.

The problems with this position are, to me, obvious.

"Only what is scientifically proven is really knowledge." Remember, what defines science is mathematical notation and experimental verification. So, how can it be experimentally verified that *only what is experimentally verified* is really knowledge? And how would you express that mathematically? Obviously, any answer to the former question would be circular, and any answer to the latter is impossible by definition.

Back to Your Mom

But let me re-quote a few things Krauss claims in his introduction: "I take a rather flippant attitude toward this concern, because I don't think it adds anything to the productive discussion, which is 'What questions are actually answerable by probing the universe?'" I hope you noticed the complex question and the false dichotomy there: "Do you want to ask where everything came from or do you want to ask something *actually answerable*?" Where exactly is the experimental evidence and the mathematical equation proving that "Where did everything come from" is an *unanswerable question*? In fact, Krauss offers none, since none can be offered. Even worse: "I discount this aspect of philosophy here because I think it bypasses the really interesting and answerable physical questions associated with the origin and evolution of our universe." I ask another question: Since when did asking one question "bypass" another? Why on earth (or anywhere else in the multiverse) can't we ask both?

I'll warn you. Krauss is the cream of the crop. Richard Dawkins spares no hyperbole, in fact, when writing the Afterword to his book:

And now we can read Lawrence Krauss for what looks to me like the knockout blow. Even the last remaining trump card of the theologian, "Why is there something rather than nothing?" shrivels up before your eyes as you read these pages. If *On the Origin of Species* was biology's deadliest blow to supernaturalism, we may come to see *A Universe from Nothing* as the equivalent from cosmology. The title means exactly what it says. And what it says is devastating.[10]

I found nothing "devastating" in Krauss's argumentation, and I hope to make that clear in this chapter. On the contrary, Krauss simply sneaks and name-calls his way out of answering the toughest questions. This dodge is especially disappointing considering the title of his book is *A Universe from Nothing: Why There Is Something Rather Than Nothing.* That is exactly the question that Krauss calls "unanswerable," and completely avoids answering, deriding those who insist on asking it because they go against his personal tastes in what is interesting and useful. This is, according to Richard Dawkins, the New Atheism's "knockout blow." That would be quite convenient for the theist, because on the question of God, it's utterly disappointing. I'll have a lot more to say about Krauss (and a few others like him) later, so this is only by way of introduction. For the record, I still enjoy his books quite a bit.

The last evasion to the question I'll present, before examining the argument itself, is to deny that it's a question at all. Take this passage from Victor Stenger:

---

[10] Dawkins, "Afterword," in Krauss, *A Universe from Nothing*, 191.

If the laws of physics follow naturally from empty space-time, then where did that empty space-time come from? Why is there something rather than nothing? This question is often the last recourse of the theist who seeks to argue for the existence of God from physics and cosmology and finds that all his other arguments fail. Philosopher Bede Rundle calls it "philosophy's central, and most perplexing, question." His simple (but book-length) answer: "There has to be something."[11]

I've got to point out the consistent phrasing of many in the New Atheism school that this is the "last recourse" of theists. Again, I'm not sure whom they're reading, but more often than not this is the very *first* thing many of us bring up. It's Stenger and Krauss and others that distract themselves with other questions until they finally get to the relevant one. But aside from that, the answer "there has to be something" is the philosophical equivalent of saying "there just is; stop asking the question." For a poignant and beautifully-written examination of this question, read Jim Holt's *Why Does the World Exist: An Existential Detective Story*. His third and fourth chapters deal more thoroughly with why simply rejecting the question won't work. His conclusion isn't theism, but I wonder if his final coin flip between "Simplicity" and "Fullness" might mean more than he thinks it does.

I don't mean to oversimplify Stenger's position as simply dismissive. He spends a lot of time in at least two of his books giving scientific descriptions of how it might happen that something could come from nothing, but more often than not he (and similarly Krauss) equivocate

---

[11] Stenger, *God: The Failed Hypothesis*, 132.

on "nothing" (to "equivocate" means to use the word in two different senses). I'll have more to say on this later.

GET TO THE POINT

Well, I'll ask the question, even if Stenger and company don't like it. Where did the world come from? In some ways, the argument for God from the Big Bang is too simple for explanation, and maybe this is where a theist could go wrong in making a difficult question out to be easier than it should be. There is nothing, then there is something, which turns into the whole universe. The turning-into-the-universe part is where science comes in, though there seems to be some disagreement about a few factors. Nevertheless, the pertinent questions regarding God as Creator of the universe (or, similarly, multiverse— more on that later) do not have to do with the *development* of the universe after the Big Bang. For all of it to be accounted for by the ordinary workings of the forces of nature would not be any kind of surprise to a theist worth his salt—we saw how the God of Aquinas's proofs is one who works through nature, not apart from it and certainly not against it. The same would go here. The First Mover moves through natural forces and agents. The Creator of the universe would develop it in the same way.

The issue is not how the universe came to be after the Big Bang happened (that is an extremely interesting topic, by the way). The issue is *what caused the Big Bang*. The amount of ink spent on the question of post-Bang development in books purporting to be about God's existence is really misleading, and I'll challenge you to do the following experiment: pick up any of the books attempting to disprove God's existence, or show evidence against it, through science (take a look at the bibliography at the end of this book for some ideas). Read through every page. Then count how many pages are dedicated to the actual question *what caused the Big Bang?* and compare it to how many pages are dedicated to the universe's development *after* the Big Bang. The proportion is overwhelmingly small, to say the least. It seems very much as if these writers have something to hide, and there is every reason to believe they are hiding the fact that they can't answer the real question at all, and so resort to red herrings (distractions from the actual argument). Like I said, the universe's development post-Big Bang is fascinating, but it's a different question.

There is nothing—not empty space, but absolute non-being. Or, there is a point-like particle not existing in any space at all. Then there is a Big Bang that produces all of space and time. The Thing that Banged is said to have been unimaginably small. But it's still something (even if it's only empty space), and to produce that infinitesimally small something out of nothing, without Divine power, is no easier than producing something the size of our galaxy, since both are completely impossible. In other words, making a smaller thing come out of nothing doesn't help the atheist's case at all. The "distance" (to use a metaphor, since that's all that works when we're referring outside of space-time) between absolute nothingness and anything at all is infinite. Multiply zero by anything and you get zero. Nothing, as the saying goes, comes from nothing. This infinite distance must have been crossed by something with infinite power.

SPACE AND TIME: NOT FOR GOD

So (to bring up an old, and I hope well-established point), does this prove that our guardian angels watch us closely and that heaven is made of cotton candy and is located seven miles above New York City? No. But that doesn't mean it proves nothing. It proves quite a bit. The universe as a whole must have come from something, and this some-thing must be something distinct from the universe. Even if the Big Bang was a Bang of an extremely small parti-cle or portion of empty space, the most obvious (not, as Stenger thinks, "last resort") question is "where did *that* come from?" To answer "it was always there" is to miss an important point (that we have partially thanks to Ein-stein): where there is no space, there is no time. "Always" doesn't have any meaning "before" the beginning.

This brings us to another point. If the cause of space itself must be outside of space (therefore, having no con-fined "location" or "extension"), the cause of time itself must be outside of time. In classical terms, this is only to say that God is immaterial and eternal. It isn't that God was sitting around in a dark space for eons and then at some point randomly decided to create the world. There was no space for him to sit around in (no chair either), and there was no time to pass for him to deliberate over his de-cision. Thinking about immateriality and eternity isn't the easiest thing to do (since our minds are built for knowing through the senses); one might say it's even impossible for us. But that doesn't affect the conclusion or the argument, just like the difficulty of thinking of time as a fourth di-mension tied to our three spatial dimensions doesn't affect whether or not it's true.

Responses: I'm Sorry for Asking

Before looking at some of the heavier objections to this argument, I'll get a few lighter things out of the way. Similar to the evasion of the argument above, the answer "the universe is just there and it's a dumb question to ask where it came from," is the "nobody knows" response. Guy Harrison, quoting Charles Seife, describes the Big Bang: "There is no space; there is no time. There is not even a void. There is nothing. In an instant, the nothing becomes something. In an enormous flash of energy, the big bang creates space and time. Nobody knows where the energy came from— perhaps it was just a random event, or perhaps it was one of many similar big bangs."[12] "Nobody knows" is an odd thing for a scientist to say, unless he's done the appropriate worldwide surveys to make sure this is true. Of course, this is hyperbole. But even as such it is exaggerated. Perhaps someone does know, and there is a clear answer, one clearer than the "random event" (another way to say "it just happened") or the "one of many similar big bangs" answers. The multiplication of big bangs that need explanation doesn't bring us any closer to an answer, of course, but only pushes the question back—where did all those many big bangs come from? This possibility is often related to one of the multiverse hypotheses, and the same objection applies to them—where did the multiverse come from? (I always found it strange that anyone would think "the multiverse" is anything like an answer to "where did the universe come from?" But more on that later.)

Harrison makes a few other mistakes when discussing

---

[12] Charles Seife, *Alpha and Omega: The Search for the Beginning and End of the Universe* (New York: Viking, 2003), 63–89, quoted in Guy P. Harrison, *50 Reasons People Give for Believing in a God*, 72.

the implications of the Big Bang. Acknowledging the idea that people often connect it with the idea of a creation, he says:

> Believers who see the big bang theory as science finally catching up to religion would do well to slow down and consider that science is still totally silent about the existence of any gods, much less a god being responsible for the big bang. Yes, some people try very hard to make that connection but they are way out of line with the evidence and do not represent the views of most cosmologists and astronomers. To date, all claims that a god has been discovered are hollow and misleading. Cosmology has not unveiled any gods, despite the statements sometimes printed on book covers and in magazine headlines.[13]

If the question at hand is whether there is a God who created the world as we see it, who created space and time from "outside" both of them, then it is no surprise at all that "science is still totally silent about the existence of any gods." Science *must* be totally silent about the question, by its very nature, if by science we mean the mathematical, experimental study of the universe. That's like saying Mozart was totally silent about the existence of ancient Sumerian tablets. They're just not his business.

Of course, once the line is crossed from experimentation and mathematical description of, for example, natural forces, to the question of where these realities came from, that becomes a question of interpretation. But interpretation is a different discipline than experimentation and

---

[13] Harrison, *50 Reasons People Give for Believing in a God*, 74.

mathematical expression—it's not what scientists are trained in. So it really makes no difference whether connecting the Big Bang to the activity of a creating God does not "represent the views of most cosmologists and astronomers." Such surveys (which are more often referred to vaguely than actually cited) are empty arguments, exposing nothing more than the opinions of people on a question outside their training. I suppose you could survey electrical engineers about the meaning of *The Brothers Karamazov*, and you might very well find something interesting; but what you'd find certainly wouldn't be the last word.

Another minor way to miss the mark is to pigeonhole the Creator's activity into a spot it was never meant to be in the first place. If we are positing a God who is outside time and space, who creates time and space, then this creative activity must also be outside time and space. An example of someone missing this point is Nicholas Everitt:

> What about the universe as a whole—could that have a cause? There is a straightforward reason for saying that the universe as a whole *could not* have a cause. Recall that the phrase "the universe" is here being used to include space and time as well as matter. This means that there *could not have been* an event preceding the universe and bringing it about, for the simple reason that there was no time before the start of the universe in which that event could have occurred.[14]

Of course the event "preceding" the universe is not an event *in time*. We are talking about natural priority, which is independent of time (remember the First and Second

---

[14] Everitt, *The Non-existence of God*, 70.

Proofs in chapter three). Looking for God's activity within time and space is like looking for buried treasure above ground. Victor Stenger makes practically the same mistake: "The four space-time symmetries described above are just the natural symmetries of a universe with no matter, that is, a void. They are just what they should be if the universe appeared from an initial state in which there was no matter—from nothing."[15] And this, I add, is exactly what it should be in a universe created by God *ex nihilo*, which means exactly "from nothing." The answer to the question, in other words, isn't here, since the evidence is exactly as it would be in either case. If something came from nothing without God, then you get XYZ. If something came from nothing with God, then you get XYZ. Stenger adds nothing.

MORE NOTHING

This brings me again to Lawrence Krauss, the New Atheism's "knockout blow." I quoted already from his introduction, where he (I think rightly) distinguishes "why" from "how," and (I think wrongly) says that the latter is the domain of science, and the former not a meaningful question. The bulk of his book is a fascinating and lucid exposition of many of the principles of theoretical physics. Finally, in chapters nine and ten, he returns to the issue of how something can come from nothing, to some degree building on the material he has presented throughout the book. It is here that the definition of "nothing" becomes a serious problem with his thought. In chapter nine, titled "Nothing is Something," he attempts to clarify his terms:

---

[15] Stenger, *God: The Failed Hypothesis*, 130.

First, I want to be clear about what kind of "nothing" I am discussing at the moment. This is the simplest version of nothing, namely empty space. For the moment, I will assume space exists, with nothing at all in it, and that the laws of physics also exist. Once again, I realize that in the revised versions of nothingness that those who wish to continually redefine the word so that no scientific definition is practical, this version of nothing doesn't cut the mustard. However, I suspect that, at the times of Plato and Aquinas, when they pondered why there was something rather than nothing, empty space with nothing in it was probably a good approximation of what they were thinking about.[16]

Every single claim in the quotation above is false or at best disingenuous. Empty space is not in any way the "simplest" version of "nothing." If his book taught me anything, it's that empty space is far from simple—it is a dynamic and fascinating thing; a far cry from "nothingness." His next sentence illustrates that nicely, in fact—he assumes space and the laws of physics exist. I'm not sure what exactly the laws of physics are, but they're certainly not nothing, especially if we speak with (I think) more precision and call them the "forces" rather than laws.

His following two statements are even worse. First, he shows that he is aware that his definition of "nothing" won't "cut the mustard," but blames this on some supposed group that wishes to "continually redefine the word so that no scientific definition is practical." I am not aware of Krauss's education in the history of thought, but the distinction between "nothing" and "empty space" is at least as old as

---

[16] Krauss, *A Universe from Nothing*, 149.

Aristotle (he has an entire section, in his *Physics*, on the notion of "void," for example), and certainly passed into medieval thought clearly in Thomas Aquinas. Saying that nothing is not empty space but rather *nothing at all* is not a "revision" of the word. Claiming that it is a revision is either, I'm sorry to say, ignorant or dishonest. I won't comment on the last sentence quoted, where he says that Plato and Aquinas would have considered empty space equivalent to nothing, except to say that he should have done more research before making a statement like that. For the record I'm sure Aristotle and Aquinas would be fascinated by the developments of modern science. Probably not Plato—he didn't seem to care much for the physical world, depending who you ask (though String Theory seems eerily similar to some ideas in his *Timaeus*, as Krauss points out in another book).

For the rest of the book, Krauss jumps back and forth between using "nothing" to mean "empty space" and admitting that empty space really isn't "nothing" after all: "Nothing required this except theoretical speculations based on considerations of a universe that could have arisen naturally from nothing, or at the very least, from *almost nothing*."[17] The emphasis is his. Krauss is aware that there is a difference between what he's talking about and "real" nothingness. Later in the same chapter he clarifies what he means: "Therefore, our observable universe can start out as a microscopically small region of space, which can be essentially empty, and still grow to enormous scales containing eventually lots of matter and radiation, all without costing a drop of energy, with enough matter and radiation to account for everything we see today!"[18] A "microscop-

---

[17] Ibid., 148.
[18] Ibid., 151.

ically small region of space" that is "essentially empty" is still infinitely distant from the pure nothingness that is at the heart of the question. Again, Krauss knows this quite well, and admits it near the end of chapter nine:

> While inflation demonstrates how empty space endowed with energy can effectively create everything we see, along with an unbelievably large and flat universe, it would be disingenuous to suggest that empty space endowed with energy, which drives inflation, is really *nothing*. In this picture one must assume that space exists and can store energy, and one uses the laws of physics like general relativity to calculate the consequences.[19]

Therefore, he implies, in the tenth chapter he will show how something can come, not from empty space, but from absolute nothingness.

MOST NOTHING

It all comes down to this. Unfortunately for Krauss's case, the tenth chapter, titled "Nothing is Unstable," isn't what he needs it to be. The case he eventually presents rests on a theory of quantum gravity that doesn't exist, and (by his own admittance in other works) might not ever exist. This theory would require a unification of general relativity with quantum mechanics, two theories which are not, in Krauss's words, "fully consistent."[20] This is quite an understatement. Unifying these two theories is so complex that String The-

---

[19] Ibid., 152.
[20] Ibid., 162.

orists (as one example of such an attempt) have needed to posit up to twenty-six dimensions in order to make mathematical sense of all the known forces in the universe.

But I'm getting ahead of myself. You can tell how weak Krauss's tenth chapter is by observing his need to constantly use vagaries to water down his claims: "On these scales, gravity must be treated as a fully quantum mechanical theory, and our current understanding of general relativity is not sufficient to allow us to determine precisely what will happen";[21] "A definitive description of how this process could have happened in the early universe is currently lacking";[22] "Extending quantum mechanics to include such a possibility is tricky";[23] "But let's consider even stranger possibilities"; "by analogy"; "should one consider the possibility of small, possibly compact spaces that themselves pop in and out of existence?"; "These are open questions."[24] I am honestly impressed how many ways Krauss has of saying "this is complete conjecture." This is a different intellectual world from Aquinas's five proofs. Nothing this vacuous would have come from Aquinas.

In addition to the vagaries of the chapter, it takes Krauss almost half of it to even begin to speculate how absolute nothingness could produce something. Until then, he continues his habit from the last chapter of equating "nothing" with "empty space"[25] or even something existing in space, like a black hole,[26] or an asymmetry of matter over antimatter.[27]

---

[21] Ibid., 156.
[22] Ibid., 158.
[23] Ibid., 161.
[24] Ibid., 163.
[25] Ibid., 159.
[26] Ibid., 156.
[27] Ibid., 157.

Aside from all this, the argument itself is simply impossible. Citing Stephen Hawking, Krauss claims: "a quantum theory of gravity allows for the creation, albeit perhaps momentarily, of space itself where none existed before."[28] The picture he paints requires "the total energy of a closed universe [to be] zero,"[29] and that the extremely tiny amount of time (ten–forty-four seconds) a quantum particle could cause space to come from nothingness must also coincide with a period of extreme inflation.

I have no quarrel with any of the underlying physical theories Krauss proposes (I have neither the need nor the competence, in fact, to argue against them). I have a quarrel with the very possibility that there could be a physical theory of absolute nothingness. Even assuming that quantum gravity could one day be a workable theory, it is impossible that *any* physical theory could ever apply to absolute nothingness. For a "law" to exist, or a "force" to work, or anything to "happen" in any way, time and space are an absolute prerequisite; if any law, or force, or happening, could exist, then space and time already exist beforehand. If quantum gravity applies to it, then it's not nothingness you're talking about. *Where* would this event occur or this force be applied when there's no space? *When* would this event occur or this force be applied where there's no time? Victor Stenger, realizing this, will retract the premise that the Big Bang implies a beginning of space and time at all, and thereby attempt to avoid the whole question of something coming from nothing. Before examining his case, however, one last word on Krauss's argument.

What follows is Krauss's conclusion regarding the question of something coming from nothing, which he makes

---

28 Ibid., 163–164.
29 Ibid., 167.

before turning to the question of why the forces of nature are so perfectly tuned (which he escapes by positing a multiverse, which I will deal with later in this chapter). This selection is found on pages 174–175 of his book, and I will make a few comments after each paragraph:

> The metaphysical "rule," which is held as an ironclad conviction by those with whom I have debated the issue of creation, namely that "*out of nothing nothing comes,*" has no foundation in science. Arguing that it is self-evident, unwavering, and unassailable is like arguing, as Darwin falsely did, when he made the suggestion that the origin of life was beyond the domain of science by building an analogy with the incorrect claim that matter cannot be created or destroyed. All it represents is an unwillingness to recognize the simple fact that nature may be cleverer than philosophers or theologians.

This first premise of his concluding argument, that there is "no scientific foundation" for the claim "out of nothing nothing comes," is utterly false. As I showed above, this is simply an equivocation on the word "nothing," and nothing more. Even as such, it doesn't assume that something can come from nothing—even from empty space. The particles that pop out of empty space do so not because that's what "nothing" does, but because that is the very nature of space-time, and science is pursuing the question of how (and maybe even why) this happens because it assumes that something does *not* come from nothing. If it was really believed that "something could come from nothing," science would simply stop.

At this point Krauss turns to theology proper:

Moreover, those who argue that out of nothing nothing comes seem perfectly content with the quixotic notion that somehow God can get around this. But once again, if one requires that the notion of true nothingness requires not even the *potential* for existence, then surely God cannot work his wonders, because if he does cause existence from nonexistence, there must have been the potential for existence. To simply argue that God can do what nature cannot is to argue that *supernatural* potential for existence is somehow different from regular natural potential for existence. But this seems an arbitrary semantic distinction designed by those who have decided in advance (as theologians are wont to do) that the supernatural (i.e., God) must exist so they define their philosophical ideas (once again completely divorced from any empirical basis) to exclude anything but the possibility of a god.

This is the same trick Dawkins used when dealing with Aquinas's Five Proofs: reading the proof backwards. It's not that because we want to believe in God and are desperate to prove him that we posit that "God can get around this." It's that there is no natural way to explain nature's existence, and so we are forced by reason to turn to something supernatural; there's no natural law that could ever explain the Big Bang, and so we look beyond nature by the logic of the question itself. As for God being able to do something that nature can't, and bringing something into existence without even the potential for existence being there beforehand, I remind you that this is a very different question, and one that I think is really interesting. For more on it, look at Aquinas's *Summa Theologica* I, question 45.

"Does It Have to Be This Way?" I Don't Know, Timmy. I Don't Know.

Einstein is often quoted as wondering "whether God had a choice" in creating the universe. What he meant by this is whether the forces of nature, which are "tuned" so precisely, must have been this way, or could have been otherwise. Just how precise is the tuning? Richard Dawkins cites Martin Rees and gives one example among many:

> If the strong force were too small, say 0.006 instead of 0.007, the universe would contain nothing but hydrogen, and no interesting chemistry could result. If it were too large, say 0.008, all the hydrogen would have fused to make heavier elements. A chemistry without hydrogen could not generate life as we know it. For one thing, there would be no water.[30]

So where did this precise tuning come from? Who (this would be tongue-in-cheek in another book, I suppose) tuned it so precisely?

Here's where I'll take an opportunity to illustrate how a theological answer and a physical answer would not interfere with each other. Let's say I were to posit "God did it that way" as the answer to "Why are all the forces so finely tuned as to allow the possibility of life?" This is a theological answer, but no honest thinker would be content with this as a physical one. Aquinas could have answered any question about creation with "God did it that way," and yet that was not satisfactory for him (he wrote thousands of pages of extremely dense works discussing natural phi-

---

[30] Dawkins, *The God Delusion*, 171.

losophy). Even accepting that as an answer, one can, and should, still ask *how* God did it, and even *why*.

This returns us to Einstein's question. Did God have a choice? On the level of modern physics (and there are clear parallels in ancient natural philosophy), there are, obviously, two possible answers: yes and no. The simpler answer is no. This is just the way matter, energy, space, and time *must* have been, and if one is going to create matter, energy, space, or time, there is no other way they could be than the way they are. Every force of nature is as logically necessary as having three sides to a triangle, and so just as God (at least the God of the Catholic tradition) cannot make a four-sided triangle or a stone so big he can't pick it up (not because he's not powerful enough or not free—*it* just cannot be made), he cannot have made the Strong Force to be anything other than exactly what it is. This is the position that Hume seems to have preferred, as well as Descartes.

Knowing whether or not this is the right answer is not an issue for theology. It's not really a question about God at all—it's a question about the nature of reality. If, for example, we discover that matter cannot be any other way than it is, then the logical necessity contained in its very nature answers our question. Science hasn't discovered such necessity in the forces of nature, at least yet. If it does, then one of the reasons to posit a multiverse would quickly evaporate.

Speaking of the multiverse, this is another possible answer to Einstein's question. Did God have a choice, or could the universe have been different than it is now? A multiverse is a way of saying yes. Those who posit a multiverse (in one version of the theory at least) claim that there are an enormous number of universes, each with a slight variation in their laws. The reason ours works out so well for life isn't because it's fine-tuned. We just happen to be lucky enough to be in one of the universes that produced life and didn't disintegrate in a fraction of a second, or explode into a ball of fire leaving nothing but empty space behind. This is often called the "Anthropic Principle."

Of course, there are answers in between yes and no. It's possible that *some* of the forces of nature (like the Strong Force, or Gravity) are variable, while others (possibly, for Krauss at least, quantum mechanics) are necessary. Maybe God had some choice, but not total license. Maybe some things in nature cannot be otherwise and some can. But it was God who did it. Dennett cites Darwin himself, as well as Newton, admitting this:

> When Darwin entertains the idea that the laws of nature are designed by God, he has distinguished company, past and present. Newton insisted that the original arrangement of the universe was inexplicable by "meer natural causes" and could only be ascribed to "the Counsel and Contrivance of a Voluntary Agent." Einstein spoke of the laws of nature as the "secrets of the Old One" and famously expressed his disbelief in the role of chance in quantum mechanics by proclaiming *"Gott würfelt nicht"*—God does not play dice.[31]

Whether or not God had a choice in fashioning some of the forces or not is a question science will continue to pursue. None of these possibilities, however, have anything to do with whether or not God exists. Whether the world is fine-tuned because the world must be the way it is, or whether we just happen to be in the one world tuned this

---

[31] Dennett, *Darwin's Dangerous Idea*, 164.

way, has no bearing on the question of a Creator, and any classical theist would (or at least should) accept whatever conclusion is provided by the evidence. In either case, God is still there and still doing what he does. Mixing this question with the question of the existence of a Creator is misleading and confusing, no matter which side is doing it.

The Multiverse: More to Explain

Of course, there is a much less sophisticated argument that uses the multiverse theory. It is sometimes used not to explain simply why the forces of nature are such as they are, but also to explain where our universe came from. "Where did the universe come from? The multiverse." This is a strange argument to say the least, and its response should be obvious: Then where did the multiverse come from? This argument reminds me of Aristotle's objection to Plato's world of forms: It is, he says, "as if a man who wanted to count things thought he would not be able to do it while they were few, but tried to count them when he had added to their number."[32] In other words, if the universe is hard to explain, what would make an infinite number of universes any easier to explain? In fact, there are a lot of things to explain on top of the existence of trillions of other universes, such as why there should be variation in the laws of nature in each of them and why they aren't all the same, where such a mechanism came from, and so on. This makes the whole story so much more complicated, and while it tries to answer one question it creates a huge number of new ones. While there may be some legitimate reasons to posit a multiverse, many of the New Atheist

---

[32] Aristotle, *Metaphysics* I, pt. 9.

authors present it as an alternative to admitting that there is a Creator. It is a crime to call such desperate mental acrobatics by the name "science." One might as well posit that aliens created our world:

> A final point about believers who see their god in the big bang is that attributing the event to a super intelligent being does not necessarily have to mean it was their god who lit the fuse. It just as easily could have been the god of a rival religion or even the god of a long-extinct religion. Or maybe it was the result of an experiment conducted by technologically advanced scientists from another galaxy or universe. There is no less evidence for this than there is for someone's favored god doing it. Maybe our religions have it all wrong and it really was aliens who gave our universe its start.[33]

This passage marvelously combines many different mistakes. It pushes the question back and forces the theist to sigh and ask, "Well who created those aliens then, and their world?" It also confuses things by mixing the questions together, which is a fallacy I pointed out in the first chapter. Which God did it is an entirely different question, but it should be clear by now that some God did.

No Beginning: Whatever

But the question changes if the universe or multiverse did not start with a Big Bang. If the world always existed, if there was no beginning of time, then we return to the sit-

---

[33] Harrison, *50 Reasons People Give for Believing in a God*, 74.

uation that Aquinas found himself in, living in a universe that is observably eternal, and thus we return to his proofs, which are valid with or without a Big Bang. It is Victor Stenger, building on the later work of Stephen Hawking and presenting the cosmology of Alexander Vilenkin, who takes up the flag of the eternal universe:

> . . . the claim that the universe began with the big bang has no basis in current physical and cosmological knowledge.
>
> The observations confirming the big bang do not rule out the possibility of a prior universe. Theoretical models have been published suggesting mechanisms by which our current universe appeared from a preexisting one, for example by a process called quantum tunneling or so-called quantum fluctuations. The equations of cosmology that describe the early universe apply equally for the other side of the time axis, so we have no reason to assume that the universe began with the big bang.[34]

If you're wondering what quantum tunneling means, and what it has to do with a time axis, Stenger explains it:

> Vilenkin's scenario calls for our universe tunneling out of "nothing," which he takes to be the region of chaos that existed before the big bang. However, trying to define "nothing," as we have seen, is a contentious matter. As with the quantum fluctuation model described above, cosmic creationists simply say that Vilenkin's "nothing" is still

---

[34] Stenger, *God: The Failed Hypothesis*, 125–126.

something that exists and so does not answer the question of how the universe came into existence from "nonexistence." So, for my purposes here, I am going to avoid the issue by having our universe tunnel from "something," namely a prior universe that always existed. As we saw above, we have no reason to rule out an eternal multiverse. We can envisage an earlier universe that is more or less a mirror of ours, on the opposite side of the time axis where the origin is at $t=0$. Such a universe is not forbidden by any known principle and, furthermore, is accommodated by the same cosmological equations that we use to describe our universe. Just insert a negative t in the equations.[35]

I have no particular purpose in presenting this picture of cosmology aside from a wish to be forthright: there is a picture of the "beginning" of the universe that isn't a beginning in time or space, and therefore doesn't come strictly from "nothing" in the true sense of the word. This, as I said earlier, is no problem for Aquinas's proofs. Whether the science behind this theory is valid, what the evidence for it might be, how quantum tunneling from one mirror-universe to another might work, and what "the opposite side of the time axis" could possibly mean in reality, are questions that are not my concern. Stenger acknowledges that this theory doesn't quite have the status of other cosmological theories, but holds by it nevertheless:

> I must admit that this picture of the origin of the universe is not widely recognized. However, after being in print for several years no physicist, cos-

---

[35] Stenger, *God and the Folly of Faith*, 188.

mologist, or philosopher has yet pointed out any errors. I do not claim that this is *in fact* how the universe arose. I merely present it as a scenario consistent with all of our knowledge by which the universe occurs naturally and thereby closes a gap where a theist might want to insert God.[36]

I suppose my last comment here is similar to what Stenger says above. What purpose does this theory serve aside from closing this "gap" where we might "insert" God? What direct evidence is there for it that would make it believable? He presents this picture of a mirror universe that quantum-tunneled itself from both sides of the time-axis out of almost nothing as a "scenario consistent with all of our knowledge" (meaning that there is no evidence for it, but nothing directly contradicts it) simply to get God out of the picture. This is not science. This is building a case on non-evidence with the deliberate intention to arrive at a pre-conceived theological conclusion. The amount of desperate effort required to do this is suggestive of just how threatening a Big Bang that began time and space really is to the atheist.

WHAT KIND OF GOD IS THIS?

If we side with Krauss and what seems like the majority of scientists, and affirm that the Big Bang began time and space, and if we allow reason to take the next logical step and posit a cause of this that is outside time and space, we are forced by the facts to some further conclusions. A God

---

[36] Victor J. Stenger, *The New Atheism: Taking a Stand for Science and Reason* (Amherst, NY: Prometheus Books, 2009), 171.

who causes time to exist is *ipso facto* outside of time; this reaffirms the implication of Aquinas's First Proof, that God does not change. A God who causes space to exist is *ipso facto* apart from space; this confirms that God is immaterial. But two more conclusions can be added to these classical ideas of God's eternity and immateriality. A God who brings about the universe from nothing must be infinitely powerful—remember the "distance" between absolute nothingness and anything at all, even an unbelievably tiny portion of empty space, is infinite, and crossing this infinite "distance" requires infinite power. Finally, a God who causes, through his act of creation, all of the forces of nature, those which are measured and mathematically described by what we call "laws," must be an Intellect of some kind.

I'd like to end this chapter on that note. In a later chapter I will deal with the question of "different gods," and ask whether this God that we discovered by reasoning through our observation of the natural world is a contradiction to the God of religion. Here I will make a final point about God the Intellect who causes the forces of nature that are so refined and precise as to require the precision of mathematics for their description. Sam Harris, after making the typical "what created God" glitch, brings up another point: "If God created the universe, what created God? To say that God, by definition, is uncreated simply begs the question. Any being capable of creating a complex world promises to be very complex himself."[37] This is mirrored in many of the New Atheism books. For example, Dawkins: "Any creative intelligence, of sufficient complexity to design anything, comes into existence only as the end product of an extended process of gradual evolution."[38]

---

[37] Harris, *Letter to a Christian Nation*, 73.
[38] Dawkins, *The God Delusion*, 52.

That a creative intelligence must be "complex" is a claim that needs to be supported. Despite the best efforts of Krauss and others to show otherwise, it is impossible that something come from nothing. But if science has shown us anything, it is that something complex can come from something simple: the simple forces of gravity and electromagnetism, along with the strong and weak nuclear forces, account for all the sublime complexity of our world; the simple laws that govern evolution can account for the even more complex organization of living things. This isn't really a new idea, in fact. Anyone observing nature will see a (relatively) simple seed become a tree. Nothing cannot precede something, but simplicity can easily precede complexity, and the God of classical theism is utterly simple.

I'm aware that we don't usually imagine God as utterly simple, but that is due more to culture than to theology. We are shown pictures of a bearded old man, or given dozens of questions and answers to memorize in our catechism classes, or told that he is infinite and all-loving and wise and just and so on. None of this seems simple at first glance. Because it's a different question than God's existence, I'll point you again to Aquinas, who deals with God's simplicity immediately after his existence (*ST* I.3). Take a look at what he says about God's simplicity, as well as his other attributes, and see if it makes sense to you.

But I'll make a short caveat here and ask a question that seems to jump out at us: how can an intellect be utterly simple? Doesn't the very notion of intelligence require complexity? This also is a claim that needs to be supported, and one that I think is completely false. This isn't a place to enter into epistemology, but even a rudimentary knowledge of science gives one example to the contrary. The more we learn about nature, the simpler our ideas often become. Two centuries ago, the forces of electricity and magnetism were seen as separate; we now realize they are aspects of one and the same force, and linked also to the strong and weak nuclear forces. Gravity is still the odd man out, but there are still some scientists hopeful to find a "grand unified theory" that describes it all ("quantum gravity" is one candidate that we mentioned earlier). The progress, however, is clear: the more we understand nature, the simpler our understanding is, or at least, the simpler we expect it to be. This is a single example, but it is enough to illustrate that simplicity and intellect can very much go hand in hand—even something as admittedly complex as the human intellect. The more we understand, the simpler our understanding is. Perhaps the mind of God is further along in the same direction. Classical theism says it is, and I see no reason to reject that view.

I hope I have shown both how the Big Bang implies the existence of an eternal, immaterial, all-powerful, and intellectual Creator. Like last chapter, I hope the desperation of the New Atheists in scrambling to explain away this clear implication is another indication that there is a lot at stake here. I'll conclude this chapter by quoting Krauss one last time, and challenging everyone to follow his advice, including Krauss himself:

> If we wish to draw philosophical conclusions about our own existence, our significance, and the significance of the universe itself, our conclusions should be based on empirical knowledge. A truly open mind means forcing our imaginations to conform to the evidence of reality, and not vice versa, whether or not we like the implications.[39]

---

[39] Krauss, *A Universe from Nothing*, 139.

CHAPTER FIVE

EVOLUTION

SMART PHONES DO NOT MAKE YOU SMART

I recently saw a video on the internet of a Christian preacher "rebutting" evolution. To call it an embarrassment to the human race would be a compliment. He threw around words like "entropy" and "theory" with a shocking and deceptive confidence that he had any idea what he was talking about. The video was apparently shot with his smart phone while he was sitting in his car. This video had an enormous number of views and had been linked to thousands of other sites, with their compliments.

Contrast this with an experience I had while an undergrad. I was taking a biology class at a Jesuit university. It was a relatively big class for the school, maybe two hundred students, and the professor was one of those old Jesuits they don't make anymore, and a serious scientist. He introduced the syllabus on the first day of the course, and after he had read through the topics we would cover, a hand in the front row shot up. The professor called on the student and the young man asked, in a strained voice, whether we could discuss the topic of evolution versus religion. The poor old priest sighed visibly and restrained himself from rolling his eyes, and said "sure." A few weeks later this class came, and the professor began the lecture with words I'll never forget: "The debate about evolution is not a debate between science and religion, and never has been. It is a debate between atheists and Protestants." The face of the young man who had originally asked the question the first day of class turned a charming shade of neon pink (it having become clear by then that he hailed from some such denomination), and the rest of that day's class was as entertaining as you might imagine.

I don't mean to be anti-ecumenical by telling this story. I mean only to be honest, and to illustrate this point: the video by the preacher who showed no evidence of being literate had been seen and lauded by hundreds of thousands of people; the old priest-biologist who actually knew what he was talking about was begrudgingly listened to by a couple hundred eighteen-year-olds who needed his class for credit. Popular things aren't usually the best quality things. But they are popular, and they spread like wildfire

I HATE THIS CHAPTER

I repeat a point I've made earlier. I can't blame the average atheist for thinking that the average theist must, by reason of his creed, reject evolution. That's exactly what the majority of the media out there implies. Unfortunately, it is a false reading of theism to believe that this rejection is necessary. It is also a false reading of the Christian tradition (which I will use for illustration in this chapter), and it is a false reading of the Book of Genesis. To state my point up front I will say clearly: I am saying this unequivocally. No, I am not going to try to poke holes in evolution (or worry about the distinction between macro- and micro-evolution). Yes, I believe evolution is true. In fact, I never understood, even as a child, how any theist could ever have a problem with it.

The purpose of this chapter is to show both that a belief in evolution is not a threat to a belief in God, as well as to show that a belief in God is not a threat to a belief in evolution. It is a bit irritating that this question is so enormously popular when in fact it is so astoundingly boring. Thus, as I begin to write this chapter, I hope it turns out to be a short one.

I can make a very long story short, and my readers (if they exist) can simply skip to the next chapter if they wish. To the holy-book-based theist who feels the need to reject evolution based on theism I ask: what is the difference between God making the human race out of dirt and God making the human race out of another animal? To the atheist who feels the need to reject theism I ask: what is the difference between God providing the "laws" that would produce our universe and all its complexity and God doing this without the "laws" as his instruments?

Ok, yes, there is a lot more to say than this. I'm only illustrating here that there are two sides to this debate that I believe are both wrong in their understandings as well as their emotional aggression in this question. And I'm not alone in this belief. I can cite a handful of documents from the Vatican showing this, but I'd prefer to go back to Aquinas, both because he proves again to be a thinker of great clarity, and because he stands a few centuries too early in history to be accused of reacting to Darwin (and he cites Augustine, who lived over a millennium before Darwin). What Aquinas is attempting to do is simply interpret the book of Genesis, and he does so with an honesty that is impossible when political debates about school curricula have entered the scene. The ideas he presents are not all his own, and (as I said) some go back as far as Augustine or earlier. But this isn't a book on the history of thought, and Aquinas suffices well enough for my purposes.

THE BIBLE: SMARTER THAN SMART PHONES

Since I've already started in this direction, I'll spend the first part of this chapter responding to the anti-evolution theist. After this, I will respond to the anti-theistic evolutionist.

I don't see any reason not to start with the Bible. Whatever the story it's meant to tell, most religious monotheists have the Book of Genesis in common, and can agree it's there to tell us something, and something important. But what exactly is it trying to tell us? More specifically, what is the first chapter, often called the "Creation Story," trying to tell us?

There's a lot to say about this. The first question is that of genre—what kind of writing is this first chapter? That is, how was the human author attempting to express himself? Was he (or she) intending to write a historical narrative; or express a symbolic, even mythological story; or do something else entirely? Well, there's no way to know directly, since he's no longer around to be questioned, but our best bet is to look closely at the text itself and figure it out, based on how it's written, the language used, its structure, and other such things.

We're all basically familiar with the story. Six days, God says things and they happen, he rests on the seventh. Were we meant to read this literally? Well, I'm not going to enter the debate about the genre of the text or its historical context for many reasons; but, aside from the fact that it's not my field, sifting through commentaries on the Bible can most accurately be compared to swimming through a swamp the size of the Pacific Ocean. Instead, I will point out a few things I've noticed in the text of that first chapter of Genesis that suggest it was never intended to be read literally, and then show how this interpretation is perfectly valid within a traditional Catholic intellectual framework (my apologies to anyone that might have a different framework—I can't speak for everyone). I'll leave it to anyone interested to pursue this matter further among biblical scholars. Good luck.

I'll start with the first five verses:

In the beginning God created the heavens and the earth. The earth was without form and void, and darkness was upon the face of the deep; and the Spirit of God was moving over the face of the waters. And God said, "Let there be light"; and there was light. And God saw that the light was good; and God separated the light from the darkness. God called the light Day, and the darkness he called Night. And there was evening and there was morning, one day. (Genesis 1:1–5)

Though I'm not a biblical scholar, I do happen to teach Hebrew, and I'd love to go on a long tangent and talk about the first word of the Bible, *bereshith*, but I'll spare you that. What I want to talk about is the concept of "day."

"There was evening and there was morning, one day." There's a lot to point out here. First, it's interesting to observe how the culture that produced the book of Genesis saw a day as beginning not in the morning, or at midnight, but in the evening. There are still vestiges of this understanding in some religious rituals (like the Easter Vigil or Christmas Eve). But there's a more important question to ask. What exactly is meant by a "day" in these verses? The line quoted at the beginning of this paragraph suggests that a "day" (Hebrew *yom*) is defined as "evening" followed by "morning." In the context of the larger passage, this means that the "darkness" upon the face of the deep followed by the "light" spoken into existence by God are the "evening" and "morning" referred to in the following verses.

This is no 24-hour day. This is a symbol—darkness followed by light is what "day" means here, and not anything referring to the measurement of time. This is compounded by the fact that the sun, the only way an ancient people could have measured the 24-hour day (since it was seen as "going around" the earth), isn't created until the *fourth day*! The text itself is telling us not to read it literally; the text is establishing its own symbolism, and expects us to pay attention. A literal reading is, in this case, an unfaithful and illiterate one. As you will soon see, I'm not making a radical claim here. This interpretation of Genesis is as traditional as it gets.

God of the Gaps: Worst God Ever

There is an apparent debate today between (in the words of my old professor) "atheists and Protestants" about the "origin" of life. This is unfortunate and embarrassing; it's as if some theists, finding the evidence for evolution too convincing, need to find another spot for their God, since natural processes can explain the *development* of life so well. So they stick him in the corner as the miraculous originator of the *first* life, and cross their fingers hoping science doesn't discover how life could have originated through a natural process, just as it develops.

This is often called the "God of the Gaps." Dawkins and others point out that some theists look for holes in scientific theory (that is, things that science can't explain) and point in triumph at where their God is needed. This is as abhorrent to me as it is to Dawkins. It is anti-scientific, and underlying it is an awful, perverse hope for human thought to fail. Of course, the more successful science is, the less this Gap-God is needed. But this is not the God of the Catholic tradition (again, I can't speak for everyone here). This is certainly not the God of Aquinas, or any of his proofs, which show a God who works through nature, not against it or in some gap or corner wherever it stops operating. Even more, as I hope to show, this isn't the God of the book of Genesis. In fact, and pretty ironically, the farthest back I can trace this "God of the Gaps" is to Isaac Newton, who seemed to have needed his God to poke around where his laws weren't working right.

You Are Not a Miracle

Before I get to a few comments on the text, I need to make a clear distinction. I personally believe (along with most other Christians) that the God who created the world, the God of Genesis, the cause of the Big Bang, the First Mover, and all the other things described by Aquinas's proofs, can work miracles. But I also believe that this is not his ordinary mode of operation. Ordinarily, God works through the natural world he made. Miracles are done in reference to human beings and in the context of revealed faith, and are by definition extremely rare. This is exactly why it is misguided to expect to discover a miraculous God within the workings of nature, or through a scientific test (the kind of thing Dawkins describes in a subsection titled "The Great Prayer Experiment" in *The God Delusion*[1]). What can be discovered through human reason is the God of nature; the God of miracles is discovered through faith in revelation, which is an entirely different topic (though I will touch upon this in a later chapter).

Let's go back to the book of Genesis and take a close look a few verses later:

> And God said, "Let the waters bring forth swarms of living creatures, and let birds fly above the earth across the firmament of the heavens." So God created the great sea monsters and every living creature that moves, with which the waters swarm, according to their kinds, and every winged bird according to its kind. And God saw that it was good. And God blessed them, saying, "Be fruitful and multiply and fill the waters in the seas, and let birds multiply on the earth." And there was evening and there was morning, a fifth day. And God said, "Let the earth bring forth living creatures according to their kinds: cattle and creeping things and beasts of the earth according to their kinds." And it was so. And God made the beasts of the earth according to their kinds and the cattle according to their kinds, and everything that creeps upon the ground according to its kind. And God saw that it was good. (Genesis 1:20–25)

Genesis is clear that God created both the world and life. The question isn't *whether* God did it, but *how*. Does the book of Genesis indicate that God created life by means of

---

[1] See Dawkins, *The God Delusion*, 85–90.

a supernatural miracle, or through some natural process?

I think the wording of Genesis strongly implies the latter: "Let the waters bring forth swarms of living creatures. . . . Let the earth bring forth living creatures according to their kinds . . ." The translation here (the Revised Standard Version, for those wondering) is accurate enough for our purposes. In both of these verses, the "waters" and the "earth" are the subjects of the verbs following them, the verbs indicating the production of living things. God is speaking; he is commanding, so to speak. But it is the waters and the earth that are "bringing forth" living things. This is no direct, supernatural, miraculous intervention. This is certainly God's work (a few verses later in both cases we have "God created . . ." and "God made . . ."), but God's work within and through nature, not above or beyond it.

It is not until later (verse 26) that we have "Let us make man . . ." Here God is the subject of the verb, not water or earth. This indicates the special place the human being has in the cosmos, but the second creation account in Genesis, gives us some pause before we exalt ourselves too highly. In that account, the human being is made by God, and breathed into by the same, but originates firstly in dirt (Genesis 2:7). Actually, to be precise, the male is made of dirt, and the female made from his rib, being a step away, perhaps, from her husband's earthly origin.

I'll leave it to others to go into the rich symbolism of the creation accounts of Genesis (there's a lot to say about the name "Adam" and the Hebrew noun *adamah* which means "earth"). My point here is that the production of life, according to a decently sensitive reading of the book of Genesis, is a natural process—the waters and earth produced the sea creatures and the land animals, while the human being, though requiring more of God's direct attention, originates physically from the dirt of the ground. We shouldn't expect a supernatural miracle at the beginning of evolutionary history—at least not according to the book of Genesis.

I Like That Old-Time Religion

Is this a radical, postmodern, liberal interpretation of Genesis, a knee-jerk reaction to Darwin, an act of despair to do anything possible to salvage an antiquated and irrelevant text from the destruction of scientific inquiry? Not in the least. Earlier I showed how the first chapters of Genesis present themselves not as a historical or biological treatise but as a story indicating meaning rather than mechanism. That being the case, the mechanism should be sought elsewhere. The Bible isn't interested in biology; it's interested in things much more interesting.

This isn't my personal fancy. This interpretation of Genesis has the seal of approval of arguably the two most definitive thinkers of Western Christianity: Augustine and Aquinas. For those of you counting, Augustine lived in the fourth century AD and Aquinas in the thirteenth, fifteen and four centuries before Darwin, respectively. As I said earlier, quoting Aquinas who quotes Augustine should make my point well enough, otherwise this becomes a study in the history of thought, which is a different topic.

Let's start with the question of biblical interpretation itself. While commenting on the six days of creation in Genesis, Aquinas makes this clarification:

> I answer that, In discussing questions of this kind two rules are to be observed, as Augustine teaches (Gen. ad lit. i, 18). The first is, to hold the truth of Scripture without wavering. The second is that

since Holy Scripture can be explained in a multi-plicity of senses, one should adhere to a particular explanation, only in such measure as to be ready to abandon it, if it be proved with certainty to be false; lest Holy Scripture be exposed to the ridicule of unbelievers, and obstacles be placed to their believing. (*ST* I, q. 68, a. 1)

In other words, Scripture is true, but it can have many "senses" (what we might today call "interpretations"), and we should be ready to "abandon" an interpretation the minute it is proven to be false. Aquinas, addressing himself to believers here (and citing Augustine as an authority), warns them that if they fail to do this, they will be responsible for obstacles being placed before the faith of others.

Thomas Aquinas didn't know anything about the Big Bang. Neither did Augustine. Neither of them knew about the speed of light, and the fact that much of the starlight we see in the night sky is (from our perspective) millions of years old. Neither of them knew about the evolution of life, or its immense timescale. But without any of this, they both knew that a literalistic interpretation of the six days of Genesis needed to be, in their words, "abandoned." Their reasons for doing so aren't relevant for our purposes, but had they known what we know, they would have abandoned it all the more quickly.

So if the six days aren't literally six days, what are they? Augustine thought they were symbols of the different levels of goodness in nature, culminating in the human being. Other early authors cited by Aquinas thought each day could have represented some immense amount of time. Hardly anyone seems to have thought each day represented a period of twenty-four hours, and there is no indication that any authority in the Catholic Church ever thought it was an important question in the first place. Certainly nothing like heresy was ever attached to any side of this question. Most of the time, Aquinas simply presents what earlier writers thought and says all are fine interpretations as long as they don't contradict reason, so take your pick.

Let's take a look at Augustine's view, as quoted by Aquinas. How does Augustine interpret the "time" between the six days of the creation story?

> I answer that, It is necessary to reply differently to this question according to the different interpretations given by Augustine and other holy writers. In all these works, according to Augustine (*Gen. ad lit.* i, 15; iv, 22,34; *De Gen. Contr. Manich.* i, 5, 7), there is no order of duration, but only of origin and nature. He says that the formless spiritual and formless corporeal natures were created first of all, and that the latter are at first indicated by the words "earth" and "water." Not that this formlessness preceded formation, in time, but only in origin; nor yet that one formation preceded another in duration, but merely in the order of nature. (*ST* I, q. 69, a. 1)

Thomas is playing this as conservatively as he usually does, respecting the tradition of the Church and citing Augustine and "other holy writers." But the interpretation is far from "conservative," if our standard is the average American Southern Baptist. These venerable saints have no qualm citing Genesis and stating boldly, "there is no order of duration, but only of origin and nature." That is, the "order" of the six days isn't one of "before and after" in time, but of "better and worse" in nature. It's even more explicit a sentence later: "Not that this formlessness preceded formation in time, but only in origin." There is no apology here, no preparation for the reader or expectation of his surprise. This is just the plain old traditional way to read Genesis.

AQUINAS: ALSO SMARTER THAN SMART PHONES

But my purpose here isn't only to show that Genesis isn't traditionally read in a literal way. Aquinas gives real scientific insight that you wouldn't expect from a medieval friar. In one of his earlier, more detailed works, he says:

> The human body was not brought into actual existence in those six days, as neither were the bodies of other animals, but only in the shape of seed-forms, since God in creating the elements, planted in them certain forces or seeds, so that either by the power of God, or by the influence of the stars or by seminal propagation animals might be produced. Accordingly those things that were actually produced in those six days were created not by degrees but at the same time, while the others were brought into existence as seed-forms in their like.[2]

This is remarkable. In discussing the sixth day, where Genesis states the human being and other animals were created, Thomas distinguishes between "actual" and "potential" existence, and states unequivocally that animals were *not* brought into actual existence in a matter of days

---

[2] Thomas Aquinas, *Quaestiones Disputatae De Potentia Dei*, trans. by the English Dominican Fathers (Westminster, Maryland: The Newman Press, 1952, reprint of 1932), q. IV, a. 2.

following the beginning of creation. What was created at that early period were what Thomas calls "seed forms." His explanation of this term is beautiful: "God in creating the elements, planted in them certain forces or seeds, so that either by the power of God, or by the influence of the stars or by seminal propagation animals might be produced." Thomas's picture is that God created *matter itself* with the power to develop into life, either "by the power of God" (read this as "miracle"), "or by the influence of the stars" (read this as "through natural forces"), "or by seminal propagation" (read this today, perhaps, as "through evolutionary processes").

Aquinas would be surprised at any Christian seeking some supernatural miracle at the beginning of life in the universe in order to establish "intelligent design." He is clear enough a thinker not to make a false dichotomy between God's work and nature's work. God works through nature. God establishes the forces of nature at the beginning and lets them do their job while upholding them in existence. This is truly intelligent design. Why make the forces in the first place if you're not going to use them? Where's the intelligence in that? So I hope thinking theists give up the search for the "God of the Gaps," looking with enthusiasm for something science can't explain, or for some inexplicable flaw in the natural order. If such a thing were ever found, it would not be a victory for religion, but a failure of the Creator.

DEISM: BACK FOR REVENGE

Before moving to the atheist side of this issue, a word on deism. Deism is the belief that there is a God, but that his role is limited to creation. That is, God created the world and, according to a popular illustration, "wound it like a clock," and then let it go, never to interfere. You might wonder whether the God of the proofs found in chapter three or the Big Bang discussed in chapter four, or the development of life discussed in this chapter, is the God of the deist. I will go into more detail about this in the last chapter, but I want to make a note here that I think is important: I am making a case for a reasonable understanding of God, what used to be called "natural theology" before Hume made that term a byword.

This does not imply that there is *not* a supernatural, miraculous aspect of God that is also very real. That is the main difference between the argument for theism I am putting forward in this book and deism: deism says not only that God created the world, but it says positively that he *does not* interfere or interact with the world at all. This, like many other things we've come across, is an entirely different question that needs its own arguments, but it doesn't affect the arguments of this book. God may or may not interact with the world, but it must first be asked whether he exists at all. If he does, then the reasons to believe or not believe in his further interaction with the world need to be examined on their own.

CHICKEN OR CHICKEN?

In responding to the atheist side of this debate, I'll remind you to consider the arguments presented in the last two chapters, where it was established that nature can't "move" on its own, and that its very existence requires logically that there be something outside space and time that brings it into existence. We will see that the anti-scientific theist and the anti-theistic scientist make the same mistake—they make a false dichotomy in the very question when they ask "was this God or nature?"

Where Lawrence Krauss has his *A Universe from Nothing*, a beautiful book full of fascinating science and unfortunate bad philosophy at its most critical moments, Richard Dawkins has *The Blind Watchmaker*. It's a lucid and gripping account of the evolution of life, but it makes fatal logical mistakes at its most important moments in discussing the question of God. Similar to this, but more directly philosophical, is Daniel Dennett's *Darwin's Dangerous Idea*. All these books are like Ferraris with wooden engines. They are designed beautifully and look unbeatable, but they don't go anywhere when put to the test. For the record, "Ferraris with wooden engines" is the worst metaphor I've ever come up with.

In any case, I'll let Dawkins do his job as an evolutionary biologist and explain evolution, and I will do my job as well and critique his philosophy where it needs to be critiqued. But before anything else, I should point out that Dawkins and Dennett both fall into the same false dichotomy as the fundamentalist Christians with whom they disagree so ardently:

> Almost no one is indifferent to Darwin, and no one should be. The Darwinian theory is a scientific theory, and a great one, but that is not all it is. The creationists who oppose it so bitterly are right about one thing: Darwin's dangerous idea cuts much deeper into the fabric of our most fundamental beliefs than many of its sophisticated apologists have yet admitted, even to themselves.[3]

---

[3] Dennett, *Darwin's Dangerous Idea*, 18.

I don't think Darwin's idea is so dangerous after all. But let's look at it more closely.

I'll start with a mistake that crosses both sides of this debate, that regarding complexity:

> We are entirely accustomed to the idea that complex elegance is an indicator of premeditated, crafted design. This is probably the most powerful reason for the belief, held by the vast majority of people that have ever lived, in some kind of supernatural deity. It took a very large leap of the imagination for Darwin and Wallace to see that, contrary to all intuition, there is another way and, once you have understood it, a far more plausible way, for complex "design" to arise out of primeval simplicity.[4]

I'm not surprised that Dawkins sees complexity as an argument for theism; it is presented as such by many today. But if you're paying attention, you'd have noticed that it's not one of the classical proofs given by Aquinas. That doesn't mean it's no good, but I do think it's significant. The closest Aquinas gets to an argument from "complexity" is his Fifth Proof, the argument from "order." Remember that it is fifth because it is last, and it is last because it needs the first four to work. But aside from that, the argument is about order, and order is not the same as complexity. They are related ideas, but in classical philosophy,

---

[4]   Richard Dawkins, *The Blind Watchmaker: Why the Evidence of Evolution Reveals a Universe Without Design* (New York: W. W. Norton, 1996), xix.

"order" refers to one thing being "ordered" to another, that is, being given guidance or purpose. This is not the same as "complexity," which refers to many parts acting together as one. Like I said, they are related, but not the same.

Why is this important? Well, I don't think Aquinas would have seen complexity in itself as blatant evidence for God's activity, natural or miraculous. I think, based on texts like I showed you earlier in this chapter, Aquinas would have a very easy time imagining complexity coming from simplicity. In fact, I think anyone can imagine it. A seed is, to the imagination at least, a very simple thing, and we all watch seeds grow into trees. This is a simple example, but it illustrates my point.

There's a much more important point, however. Over and over again, Dawkins and company set up a false picture of the God they are attempting to disprove, and nowhere more clearly than in their portrayal of God as complex. Let me take Sam Harris as an example: "If God created the universe, what created God? To say that God, by definition, is uncreated simply begs the question. Any being capable of creating a complex world promises to be very complex himself."[5] I mentioned this briefly in the last chapter, but to portray any respectable theism as seeing God as "complex" is to make it clear you haven't done your homework. I've already pointed out that the Question which follows that of the Existence of God in Aquinas's *Summa Theologica* is "On the Simplicity of God." God is utterly, profoundly, totally simple, and that fact is so fundamental in Aquinas's mind that it comes directly after his Existence as a point of discussion. So every part of this debate is misguided; "complexity arising out of simplicity" is *exactly* what theism claims, and it is assumed by the classical theist just as much

---

5   Harris, *Letter to a Christian Nation*, 73.

as it is by the atheistic evolutionist. Disproving a complex God is disproving no God at all.

Back to order and complexity. I said above that Thomas and the tradition he represents would have thought of order as connected with purpose—the eye is "ordered to" seeing and the feet are "ordered to" walking (what in philosophy we might call "intentionality"). So the Fifth Proof of Aquinas observes that "things which lack knowledge, such as natural bodies, act for an end, and this is evident from their acting always, or nearly always, in the same way" (*ST* I q. 2 a. 3). The consistency of the action of "natural bodies" is what implies their acting for an end.

This is not about living things only; this is about everything. This is about what we would call the most basic forces of nature. It is their *consistency* that implies design and intelligence to Aquinas, and we saw in the previous chapter that nobody has yet shown any reason to doubt him. "Where do the forces of nature come from?" is a question consistently evaded by the writers of the New Atheism movement as unimportant, but it's the whole point. If we start off assuming that the forces of nature are independent of God and act apart from his "motion" (to use the language of the First Proof), then of course we must either force God into a "gap" to work occasional miracles, or omit him completely. But as we have seen, there is no reason to make this assumption, and every reason to think otherwise.

Simply Simplicity and the Mind of God

The origin and development of life work the same way. If life is the result of the ordinary workings of natural forces, that does not omit the need for God, but rather shows it. But the problem (to us today) is that the forces of nature seem to be so utterly simple, and we (for whatever reason) have forgotten that the God of the tradition is an utterly simple God. I repeat this point again and again because it is one completely missed by the New Atheists (as well as by many of their opponents). Observe, for example, Daniel Dennett:

> It is hard to believe that something as mindless and mechanical as an algorithm could produce such wonderful things. No matter how impressive the products of an algorithm, the underlying process always consists of nothing but a set of individually mindless steps succeeding each other without the help of any intelligent supervision; they are "automatic" by definition: the workings of an automaton. They feed on each other, or on blind chance—coin-flips, if you like—and on nothing else. . . . Can [the biosphere] really be the outcome of nothing but a cascade of algorithmic processes feeding on chance? And if so, who designed that cascade? Nobody. It is itself the product of a blind, algorithmic process.[6]

His description of Natural Selection in terms of an algorithmic process (something like a very simple computer program) seems fair enough, but he drops the ball when he describes algorithms as "mindless and mechanical." They are simple, yes, but that doesn't make them mindless; simplicity takes them one step closer to God's mind. Of course, Dennett fails to realize this simple Creator God of nature, and expects instead to find a miracle:

---

[6] Dennett, *Darwin's Dangerous Idea*, 59.

Darwin has offered us an account of the crudest, most rudimentary, stupidest imaginable lifting process—the wedge of natural selection. By taking tiny—the tiniest possible—steps, this process can gradually, over eons, traverse these huge distances. Or so he claims. At no point would anything miraculous—from on high—be needed. Each step has been accomplished by brute, mechanical, algorithmic climbing, from the base already built by the efforts of earlier climbing.[7]

As I've said, at no point would a thoughtful theist expect a miracle in the origin or development of life. On the contrary, anyone honestly reading Genesis and understanding the tradition represented by Aquinas would expect just what evolutionary science is finding: the natural forces established by God are doing their job.

But are the forces of nature as dumb as Dennett makes them out to be? Take another example from later in his book:

Love it or hate it, phenomena like this exhibit the heart of the power of the Darwinian idea. An impersonal, unreflective, robotic, mindless little scrap of molecular machinery is the ultimate basis of all the agency, and hence meaning, and hence consciousness, in the universe.[8]

Evolution establishes that there isn't a miracle needed to account for life in all its complexity, because no miracle is needed where the forces of nature can do the job on

---

[7] Ibid., 75.
[8] Ibid., 203.

their own. But on what basis can we describe these forces as "unreflective, robotic, [and] mindless"? I mentioned in the last chapter that the forces of nature are so exquisitely precise that only the language of mathematics is able to describe them with accuracy. Far from suggesting a mindlessness behind the veil of the universe, this implies a Mind of enormous magnitude. I'm not sure physicists need to speak metaphorically when they describe seeking the ultimate laws of the universe as trying to discover "the mind of God."

Richard Dawkins is less precise than Daniel Dennett, and misses the mark by a greater degree. At some points, he assumes the answer he wishes to prove:

> All appearances to the contrary, the only watchmaker in nature is the blind forces of physics, albeit deployed in a very special way. A true watchmaker has foresight: he designs his cogs and springs, and plans their interconnections, with a future purpose in his mind's eye. Natural selection, the blind, unconscious and automatic process which Darwin discovered, and which we now know is the explanation for the existence and apparently purposeful form of all life, has no purpose in mind. It has no mind and no mind's eye. It does not plan for the future. It has no vision, no foresight, no sight at all. If it can be said to play the role of watchmaker in nature, it is the *blind* watchmaker.[9]

In fact, the whole question at hand is whether the laws of nature are established by God or not. If they are, then they certainly do have purpose as well as foresight. Describing

---

[9] Dawkins, *The Blind Watchmaker*, 9.

the forces themselves does not answer this question, it only pushes it back. Again, if this is an algorithmic process (in Dennett's terminology), whether or not this algorithm has purpose depends on whether or not it was made with purpose by who or whatever made it. But the fact that it is an algorithm doesn't imply anything about purpose either way (the computer program which allows me to type this is an enormous algorithm that was made by many minds with the purpose of word processing), and the fact that natural selection is automatic doesn't disprove God any more than the fact that gravity is automatic. Our question is about the origin of these forces, not their self-consciousness. In any case, I'd wonder if Dennett, or anyone else, can give an example of an actual algorithm that we know for certain was *not* created by a mind.

BOILING IT DOWN TO NOTHING

Of course, the different sciences are related to one another, and different natural realities can be described on several different levels. We can talk about a human being as a member of a social group (in which case our science would be sociology), or as a living being (and then we'd be doing biology), or as a grouping of interacting molecules (chemistry), or as a collection of fundamental particles (physics). Even more interestingly, the very principles of one science can often be understood in terms of another. Dennett says it nicely:

> After all, societies are composed of human beings, who, as mammals, must fall under the principles of biology that cover all mammals. Mammals, in turn, are composed of molecules, which must obey the

laws of chemistry, which in turn must answer to the regularities of the underlying physics.[10]

Dennett, in fact, spends a large portion of his book describing such "non-biological" realities as morality in terms of evolutionary science.

But the whole question is, where did these fundamental forces come from? We dealt with that in some detail in the previous chapter, and with the evasiveness of the whole New Atheism group. I quote again Richard Dawkins who describes the fine-tuning of nature:

> If the strong force were too small, say 0.006 instead of 0.007, the universe would contain nothing but hydrogen, and no interesting chemistry could result. If it were too large, say 0.008, all the hydrogen would have fused to make heavier elements. A chemistry without hydrogen could not generate life as we know it. For one thing, there would be no water.[11]

The question about God is a question about the ultimate explanation of these forces, and it's exactly here that the New Atheists avoid the whole question. Dawkins, apparently, is too busy to answer it:

> Physicists, of course, do not take iron rods for granted. They ask why they are rigid, and they continue the hierarchical peeling for several more layers yet, down to fundamental particles and quarks. But life is too short for most of us to follow

---

[10] Dennett, *Darwin's Dangerous Idea*, 81.
[11] Dawkins, *The God Delusion*, 171.

them. For any given level of complex organization, satisfying explanations may normally be attained if we peel the hierarchy down one or two layers from our starting layer, but not more.[12]

I think most of us can agree that life is short, but it seems proper to make the effort to dig more than "one or two layers" when one is writing books on the supposed non-existence of God. Or, if you're not willing to make that effort, don't make conclusions that require it. The closest Dennett gets to answering this question is to make the same mistake Krauss makes, and confuse the meaning of "nothing":

> What does need its origin explained is the concrete universe itself, and as Hume's Philo long ago asked, Why not stop at the material world? *It*, we have seen, does perform a version of the ultimate boot-strapping trick; it creates itself *ex nihilo*, or at any rate out of something that is well-nigh indistinguishable from nothing at all. Unlike the puzzlingly mysterious, timeless self-creation of God, this self-creation is a non-miraculous stunt that has left lots of traces.[13]

I don't expect Dawkins to know why we can't "stop at the material world" when asking about questions of causality, but I would have expected Dennett, a trained philosopher, to know the basic premises of Aquinas's proofs, and to understand that "whatever moves is moved by another."

---

[12] Dawkins, *The Blind Watchmaker*, 20.
[13] Dennett, *Darwin's Dangerous Idea*, 185.

SCIENCE AND RELIGION, SITTING IN A TREE

To conclude this chapter, I'd like to address the accusation against religion that was brought forward at the beginning of this chapter, that is, that religion is an enemy of science. What religion might or might not cause is a topic discussed in the last chapter, and the history behind the trial of Galileo is a different topic than that of this book (though, before concluding from his case that the Catholic Church discourages science, remember that the father of genetics was a Catholic monk, and the originator of the Big Bang theory was a Catholic priest). But without getting into history at all, we should ask the question: does the belief in God in itself in any way hinder science?

To realize that we can reason our way all the way to the Creator beginning with our senses is a strong affirmation not only of the power of our minds but also of the rationality of the universe. Our world makes sense from bottom to top, and only if this is the case can science reach the knowledge it seeks. Belief in God, as such, does not hinder science in any way; on the contrary, it urges reason to continue through the natural world to its ultimate Cause. And this affirmation of reason is more rational than any skepticism available, from that of Pyrrho to that of Hume, because it does not assign any arbitrary stopping point to reason's domain. If we can make sense of the objects around us, our lives and relationships, if we can measure the symmetries of nature and make predictions or state probabilities to enormous degrees of precision in almost any event in the universe, if we can (as we claim to be able to do) guess what the temperature was a hundred thousandth of a second after the Big Bang, then why should our rationality stop there and not reach the Creator, at least in some way?

This attitude is fundamental both to science and to any

rational theism. But it is not fundamental to atheism. On the contrary, many atheists would prefer to amputate the power of human reason or the knowability of the universe rather than accept the arguments for God's existence like those discussed in chapter three. This seems, at root, to be one of Hume's central theses, but I'll give you a more contemporary example in Richard Gale:

> It is imposing on the nontheist opponent of these arguments to ask him or her to grant that every true contingent proposition (or some restricted set of them) actually has an explanation; for this, in effect, is to grant that the universe is rational through and through. And this occupies almost as high an echelon in one's wish book as does the existence of God.[14]

Gale is saying that the belief in a completely rational universe, as much as a belief in God, is wishful thinking. I disagree. I think it is more rational to "grant that the universe is rational through and through" than to flip a coin to decide where its rationality ceases. But this isn't my personal belief. It is the basic premise of all science, and of any possibility for science. It's not that behind the idiotic forces of nature is an empty and uncaring void; it's that nature is so fascinatingly precise in everything it does that it demands an Author worthy of it. The truth is that God's intelligence is so overflowing that even the dumbest particle in the universe is guided by forces that require an Einstein to discover; opposite this truth is a lie that

---

[14] Richard M. Gale, "The Failure of Classical Theistic Arguments," in ed. Michael Martin, *The Cambridge Companion to Atheism* (New York: Cambridge University Press, 2007), 95.

there is "nobody there," and that therefore there's nothing to understand. In principle, it is science and atheism that are enemies, not science and religion. I discussed some irrational theists at the beginning of this chapter that are among the many exceptions to this principle, but this is a result of their irrationality, not their theism.

CHAPTER SIX

EVIL

I'm Sorry for Being a Jerk

Remember at the beginning of the book there were two core objections to God's existence: first, that the world can be explained without him; second, that there is evil in the world and that doesn't seem to be compatible with a Good God. The past three chapters have been mostly about the first objection. This chapter is about the second one. But before I get into that, a word of warning.

The title of this book is *Thoughtful Theism: Redeeming Reason in an Irrational Age*. The first word in the title is meant to contrast with a lot of other possibilities—"thoughtless," for example. But one thing it will have to contrast with in this chapter is "emotional." The Problem of Evil, as it's called, seems to me at its root an emotional, not an intellectual, problem. Yes, it is a serious objection to the existence of God that needs an answer, but in my experience, the real issue with most people is not "evil" as an abstract idea that seems to object to a good Creator, but personal suffering; and it's hard, if not impossible, for a person to be completely cool and objective in the face of personal suffering.

That being said, I need to warn anyone reading this chapter that I won't be mincing words. There is a nice way to say everything I plan on saying here, but I'm not going to say things nicely. I'm going to say them bluntly. It's not because I want to be mean, but because I want to deal with evil as an objection to God's existence, not as something that has hurt you personally. That is a matter for counseling, which I do plenty of as well. It's just not the topic of this book. So, nothing personal.

Back to Objection 1

I'm also going to speak bluntly because the objection is a blunt one. It's been reformulated hundreds of times over the centuries, but here's the way Hume says it, again through his character Philo:

> Is [God] willing to prevent evil, but not able? then is he impotent. Is he able, but not willing? then is he malevolent. Is he both able and willing? whence then is evil?[1]

Strictly speaking, this is not an objection to God in the sense of the Prime Mover, or First Cause, or Necessary Being. This is, if anything, an objection to the Fourth Proof, that of the ultimate Good. The Deist doesn't have any problem with evil, since his God doesn't care about us anyway, and isn't "good" in any meaningful sense. But it is a problem for traditional theists like Aquinas, and for anyone with a "revealed" religion or a "personal" God.

Aquinas's answer to this objection is characteristically concise:

---

[1] Hume, *Dialogues Concerning Natural Religion*, pt. X.

As Augustine says (Enchiridion xi): "Since God is the highest good, He would not allow any evil to exist in His works, unless His omnipotence and goodness were such as to bring good even out of evil." This is part of the infinite goodness of God, that He should allow evil to exist, and out of it produce good (*ST* I, q. 2, a. 3, ad. 2).

God allows evil in order to produce some greater good. On some level this is easy enough to imagine: the rain ruins the picnic but waters the crops; the animal dies and other living beings find sustenance in its body.

I'm Sorry the World Doesn't Revolve Around Bertrand Russell

But in the end, is it all worth it? Or, phrased differently, does the balance of good and evil tip toward some evidence of a loving God in the end, or not? Bertrand Russell thinks not:

When you come to look into this argument from design, it is a most astonishing thing that people can believe that this world, with all the things that are in it, with all its defects, should be the best that omnipotence and omniscience have been able to produce in millions of years. I really cannot believe it. Do you think that, if you were granted omnipotence and omniscience and millions of years in which to perfect your world, you could produce nothing better than the Ku Klux Klan or the Fascists?[2]

---

[2] Russell, "The Argument from Design" in *Why I Am Not a Christian*, 10.

I suppose, in passing, someone could answer Russell and point out that, in fact, God has produced plenty of things better than the KKK and the Fascists, but that is beside the point. The point is, Bertrand Russell does not approve. One could here become especially snarky and ask when God asked for his approval in the first place, and what gives him, an imperfect being who exists and (according to his own belief system) ceases to exist in the blink of an eye (cosmologically speaking), any right to think he can judge the relative good and evil in the big scheme of things. Hume, speaking again through Philo, seems to me to even satirize the point Russell makes seriously:

> A being, therefore, who knows the secret springs of the universe might easily, by particular volitions, turn all these accidents to the good of mankind and render the whole world happy, without discovering himself in any operation. A fleet whose purposes were salutary to society might always meet with a fair wind: Good princes enjoy sound health and long life: Persons born to power and authority be framed with good tempers and virtuous dispositions. A few such events as these, regularly and wisely conducted, would change the face of the world; and yet would no more seem to disturb the course of nature or confound human conduct than the present economy of things, where the causes are secret and variable and compounded.[3]

At some point, the problem of evil just gets absurd: not only does the objector expect their Good God to miraculously intervene any time someone they dislike wins an

---

[3] Hume, *Dialogues Concerning Natural Religion*, pt. XI.

election, but they expect him to adjust the winds so that their ships can make it to harbor without inconvenience. This is beginning to look less like a Good God and more like a pusillanimous waiter, desperately bringing us anything we might desire so we can give him the honor of believing in him. If this is the God the New Atheists expect, I don't blame them for not wanting to worship him. I wouldn't even talk to him.

But to deny the existence of God on a basis like this reveals much more about the person denying than about the God denied. That God doesn't immediately bow to every one of my wishes or suspend the forces of nature whenever it is convenient for me is exactly what any of us should expect. But seeing this basic reality and concluding "there is no God" is equal to saying "I can't imagine a God who doesn't make the universe revolve around me." To call this "narcissism" would be an unjust compliment. St. Augustine says it smartly: "Something very similar to this is found in the case of uninstructed men who, on account of their feeble mentality, are unable to grasp and to study the integral fittingness of things. They think that the whole universe is disarranged if something is displeasing to them, just because that thing is magnified in their perception."[4]

Something Serious

But what if the example of evil isn't so trite? What happens when the evil is something inescapably horrifying? Dostoevsky, speaking through Ivan in *The Brothers Karamazov*, gives this example:

---

[4] Augustine, *On Order* I, debate 2.

"This poor child of five was subjected to every possible torture by those cultivated parents. They beat her, thrashed her, kicked her for no reason till her body was one bruise. Then, they went to greater refinements of cruelty—shut her up all night in the cold and frost in a privy, and because she didn't ask to be taken up at night (as though a child of five sleeping its angelic, sound sleep could be trained to wake and ask), they smeared her face and filled her mouth with excrement, and it was her mother, her mother did this. And that mother could sleep, hearing the poor child's groans! Can you understand why a little creature, who can't even understand what's done to her, should beat her little aching heart with her tiny fist in the dark and the cold, and weep her meek unresentful tears to dear, kind God to protect her? Do you understand that, friend and brother, you pious and humble novice? Do you understand why this infamy must be and is permitted? Without it, I am told, man could not have existed on earth, for he could not have known good and evil. Why should he know that diabolical good and evil when it costs so much? Why, the whole world of knowledge is not worth that child's prayer to 'dear, kind God'! I say nothing of the sufferings of grown-up people, they have eaten the apple, damn them, and the devil take them all! But these little ones!"[5]

The suffering of children is, for the reasons Ivan explains, the evilest of evils, and so if we are going to really face the

---

[5] Fyodor Dostoevsky, *Brothers Karamazov*, trans. Richard Pevear and Larissa Volokhonsky (New York: Everyman's Library, 1992), 241–242.

question, this is the face the question must take on—the face of a suffering child. This is a different story entirely than the examples of political elections and favorable winds cited above from Hume and Russell. Victor Stenger quotes a website run by Evan Fales, who expresses this dramatically:

> But God is not hiding out of solicitude for our freedom. We have not forgotten Job: therefore we understand that God is hiding out of cowardice. God is in hiding because He has too much to hide. We do not seek burning bushes or a pillar of smoke. No—we wish to see God. Can God stand before us? Can God see the face of suffering humanity—and live?[6]

This quote is expressive of the problem at hand because it cleverly reverses the biblical image of humanity being unable to see the face of God and live—an image meant to express the majesty of God in comparison with created beings.

Is this a reasonable image? Does it make sense—according to reason, not emotion—to imagine God as having to answer to us, even for the most horrific events? Even in the case of a personal God, no. We are speaking of a being of infinite power, one who is the cause of the entire universe, from every force to every particle to space and time themselves. We are not complaining against our neighbor building a shed on our property without our permission; there is no proportion between us, and no answer

---

[6] Evan Fales, "Despair, Optimism, and Rebellion," The Secular Web, https://infidels.org/library/modern/evan_fales/despair.html, quoted in Stenger, *God: The Failed Hypothesis*, 241.

required. Not according to reason. Emotion here needs simply to be put in check. The Old Testament expresses this idea at the end of the book of Job. This idea, in fact, is the whole message of that book, and as much as the book of Job has been mocked and misrepresented, its message is one that is supremely reasonable. After nearly forty chapters of complaints and explanations from Job and his idiot friends, ". . . the LORD answered Job out of the whirlwind:"

"Who is this that darkens counsel by words
    without knowledge?
Gird up your loins like a man,
I will question you, and you shall declare to me.
"Where were you when I laid the foundation of
    the earth?
Tell me, if you have understanding.
Who determined its measurements—surely you
    know!
Or who stretched the line upon it?
On what were its bases sunk,
or who laid its cornerstone,
when the morning stars sang together,
and all the sons of God shouted for joy?" (Job
    38:1–7)

Like I said, this chapter might be a little harsh.

LET ME TELL YOU A STORY

I remember being on a train with some friends, one of whom was struggling intensely with his belief in God, and specifically with the problem of evil. We decided to go to a quiet car toward the back of the train and talk it out. The friend in question is a very intelligent and kind man, and grew up in an exceptionally religious Catholic family. I remember his objections being sincere and well-formulated, and our discussion being intense but never angry. At some point in the discussion, while I was attempting to explain how God can bring good out of evil, and he was objecting that my explanation didn't make sense to him, I responded: "Is it reasonable to think that God's activity would always make sense to us?"

It has been about a decade since that conversation, and I realize now how potentially dangerous my question was. I meant it, and I still think there is a deep truth in it, but it needs to be said more clearly than I said it that day. Left vague, my question implies the possibility that God is, or could be, utterly disconnected from rationality. I certainly didn't mean it that way, but in the ten years since that train ride, I've understood just how dangerous an irrational God can be, and therefore choose my words more carefully, lest I imply such a God in any way.

What I meant when I said that, and what I want to say now, is that it is unreasonable to think that God's activity would *always* make sense to us—stress on the "always." Without this stress, we are left with the God of Ockham, who is beyond even the laws of logic. We are left with a God who can create a square circle, an immortal mortal, a free will that can be forced to choose. On the contrary, the God we find in Aquinas and related thinkers (including Pope Benedict XVI in our day) is a God who is supremely rational—a God who is *logos*, which is a Greek word meaning "word" but also "reason."

With this clarification (I hope) clearly made, I can explain what I meant to say on that train. If an adult has a hard time explaining something to a toddler—why, for example, she must undergo some surgery—then perhaps there are things that God cannot make us understand, as much as he might try. This is not because these things are irrational, but because we cannot see everything he sees. All the pain of the surgery might be completely necessary for that little girl, but she doesn't have the capacity yet to understand why. Perhaps the pain we feel, the darkness we discover all over the world, is not irrational but simply beyond our localized vision and partial understanding. Perhaps God knows more than we do, in a proportion infinitely greater than that between us and that toddler. In fact, it would be irrational if it were not so. It is unreasonable to think we could understand everything the way God understands it.

Speaking for God: Stop It

Does this make the pain any more bearable? Not really, but this chapter isn't about making the pain bearable. It's about answering an objection to God's existence. We can figure out quite a bit in our world, but I don't know why everything happens the way it does. I can't know. Neither can you. And that is not unreasonable, considering the kinds of minds in question. But this brings me to one of my deepest pet peeves—more than that, it's something that makes me completely furious. Whenever some national or international tragedy occurs—for example, when a hurricane hits a city—it's just a matter of time before some TV evangelist pretending to represent some religion or another (in America it's usually Christianity) goes on the air and explains to the rest of us why God did what he did. Generally, it has to do with the sins committed in that city, or the fact that the wrong politician was elected.

This monstrous arrogance is a deeper aberration even

than the narcissism I discussed earlier in this chapter. Here you're not upset because God doesn't explain himself to you; you're happy because God has obeyed you. In case there's some doubt whether this attitude is authentic in Christianity, and in case the thunderstorm of God's answer to Job wasn't enough, we can bring Jesus into the picture:

> There were some present at that very time who told [Jesus] of the Galileans whose blood Pilate had mingled with their sacrifices. And he answered them, "Do you think that these Galileans were worse sinners than all the other Galileans, because they suffered thus? I tell you, No; but unless you repent you will all likewise perish. Or those eighteen upon whom the tower in Siloam fell and killed them, do you think that they were worse offenders than all the others who dwelt in Jerusalem? I tell you, No; but unless you repent you will all likewise perish." (Luke 13:1–5)

People ask Jesus about some other people who were murdered, and whether this happened to them as a punishment for their sins. Jesus answers an unequivocal "no." He brings up another example of a kind of "natural disaster" of a tower that fell and asks his audience the same question, answering it again with a clear, resounding "no." In both cases, Jesus adds the phrase "unless you repent, you will all likewise perish." The sins of others and the tragedies that befall them are not our business to understand; our own sins are.

So do everyone a favor and stop interpreting God's will. It was never your job and it never will be. In fact, when we back off like this, things often make a lot more sense. My friend back on that train asked me about the

Holocaust (in fact, I believe the train was just then leaving Poland and we had just visited Auschwitz), and asked how he could believe in God knowing that that had happened. I answered (as I always do) that I don't know. But I pointed out that some of the people who were there, who had survived the Holocaust, still believed in God. The evil had hurt them directly; it wasn't an abstract concept or something they had read in a book, and they still believed. What excuse did he have?

GOD, WHERE ARE YOU? OH.

As easily as the book of Job is dismissed, its main lesson is one we seem to need more than ever: God is not a buddy who either owes us an explanation or whose motives are ours to explain. But there's more to be said than simply "shut up and accept it." Let's look at the question, "Where is God when bad things happen to good people?" and try to answer it as reasonably as we can.

There are two important distinctions to make. First is the distinction between God's action in nature and his action through miracles. When we ask "where is God?" the primary answer in every case is "he is outside time and space creating the world." Every particle is dependent upon God for its existence, as are the forces of nature. Without him holding them in being, they and the whole universe would cease to exist instantaneously. This is more or less implied by the material in chapter three.

Within this creative act, the forces of nature, the working of space-time, and everything up to human free will, are counted as given, standard realities that are there whether we like it or not. Could God have created a world where the strong force of the nucleus was one ten-thousandth weaker or stronger? Perhaps, but that would have resulted in a world with no life. He chose to create a world with life. Could God have created a world with life but with no consciousness or free will? Yes. But he chose to create this one, for better or for worse. In a world with no life, there at least would have been no death. In a world with no free will, there at least would have been no sin. But that isn't our world, and it was never our choice to begin with. It was always his choice, and arguing with the Creator about how he should have created when we only learned to tie our shoes a few years ago is unreasonable to the point of absurdity. The beginning of wisdom is to just grow up and accept that the world is the way it is, and then go on from that starting point.

CALM DOWN WITH THE MIRACLES

Here's where I empathize with Ivan Karamazov. I have, with a broken heart, counseled dozens of people that were molested, abused, or raped as children or as adults. God created a world where the forces of nature work with regularity, and a world where free will is free, and the results are that these people were hurt terribly. If I were to balance it, I might vote that it were better not to create a world at all if this were the result, or create a world without life or free will. But I didn't get a vote, and that makes perfect sense because I don't see anything close to the big picture. God didn't ask my advice when he created the world, and he didn't need it. If I see that the balance is tipped and it all wasn't worth it, he thinks it was, and he's smarter than I am.

It's also self-centered for me or anyone to have expected God to suspend the fabric of the universe every time anything evil occurred. That is either asking the world to revolve around you, or again asking free will to be obstructed. Miracles, if they exist (I believe they do but haven't discussed them directly) are a secondary mode of God's activity, and a very distant second. In fact, I'd argue that miracles are third, but more on that later. A miracle, according to one version at least, is when the ordinary working of nature is supervened for the sake of something else (generally for establishing the faith, or something related to that). They are not "freebies" or song requests for the Divine DJ to play for us.

It's very important to understand that by their very nature, miracles are extremely rare. I am certain I have never witnessed one, and I don't expect to. I think people's imprecision in using the word "miracle" for everyday events that can be easily explained otherwise is harmful and scandalous, and is another one of my pet peeves (I suppose I have a lot of them). Of course, just because something isn't a miracle doesn't mean it isn't God's work—remember his primary activity is in creating nature. As you know from chapter five, I don't believe that life is, strictly speaking, a "miracle." It came about through ordinary, natural processes. But nobody talks about that because they are caught up in political debates about the curriculum of public schools.

It is here, within the issue of miracles, that the problem of evil becomes the most stark. Could God miraculously intervene every time any bad event occurs—every tornado, every murder, every tyrant? Yes he could. Would it cost him anything to do so? No it wouldn't. Why doesn't he then? I don't know. But I do know that he doesn't need to answer to me, and he doesn't owe me anything. On the contrary, he gave me everything I have, and he did the same for you. The debt is entirely on our side.

PRAYER

That being said, one might ask why we religious people pray. Prayer, as I understand it, is primarily to thank God for creating us, and secondarily to ask for the strength for ourselves and others to be instruments of good in the world (this is "grace," and completely outside the scope of this book). Praying for a miracle is allowed, but I don't generally recommend it. It just seems bratty: "Please, God, I know you're using infinite power to create the entire universe right now, but I need you to suspend the forces of nature and rip into the fabric of space-time because I would like a sunny day for my picnic tomorrow." Even worse (and this applies more directly to many of our questions) is asking God to do something that is a logical impossibility. Miracles are one thing, since the forces of nature are his creation in the first place. But God can't make a square circle, because it can't be made, and he can't force a being with free will to choose a certain way. Forced freedom is like a square circle: it can't exist. To answer an old question very simply: God can't make a stone so heavy that he can't lift it. Square circles, forced freedom, and God-proof stones are all logically impossible, and the God of traditional theism is *Logos*—reason itself.

YOU DO SOMETHING

One thing I've already alluded to is the idea of being God's instrument of good in the world. This is entering the topic of religion proper, but a word on it won't hurt as I conclude this chapter. Just as God works through the forces of nature and the world he created, he can work through human instruments. Thus, in between the two activities of creation and miracle is the activity of God by means of human beings. This is where I completely agree with the statement not to wait around for God to do something, but do it yourself. That's exactly how God might want to work—through us. To sit around praying for a miracle when we could just do something ourselves is analogous to a lazy child calling his mother from the kitchen to get him the remote control that is sitting two feet away from him. Get off your rear-end and get the remote yourself.

The same goes, I believe, for bringing good into the world. Those of us who pray should do so knowing that God wishes to answer our prayers through us. Ivan Karamazov brought up the objection of suffering children to his brother Alyosha, but he did nothing in the novel to help anyone, especially children. In fact, it was the religious Alyosha who took the time to help the children in their town, while his atheist brother Ivan found some strange enjoyment reading and collecting articles about children who had suffered. Maybe instead of wasting all his time fighting with God, he could have helped some people instead.

CHAPTER SEVEN

RELIGION

DIFFERENT GODS?
AN EXCURSUS ON SAL'S METALLICA SHIRT

Imagine having a friend who visited your house every Thursday punctually at 7 p.m., and who wore the same grey suit and blue tie every time he visited. Imagine you never saw him outside these visits, and that every memory you had of this friend was on Thursday nights in your living room, with him wearing the grey suit and blue tie. I suppose the friend needs a name, so let's call him Sal. One day, you're at the grocery store on a Tuesday at 5 p.m., and you get the shock of your life. A strange man taps you on the shoulder, and you turn around and see someone who resembles your friend Sal, but:

1. He's wearing bright red sweat pants and a faded black Metallica t-shirt, and definitely not a grey suit or blue tie;

2. He's at the grocery store with seventeen boxes of Pop Tarts in his cart, and definitely not in your living room;

3. It's Tuesday at 5 p.m. and definitely not Thursday at 7 p.m.

You conclude, based on these facts, that this must be some imposter, some phantom or zombie disguising itself as Sal but doing a bad job of it.

Your conclusion would, of course, be hilariously unlikely. Imagine the conversation that would follow this conclusion:

> SAL: Hey [insert your name here].
> YOU: Can I help you?
> SAL: It's me, Sal.
> YOU: I'm sorry, you must be mistaken.
> SAL: What?
> YOU: You can't be Sal.
> SAL: I'm pretty sure I know who I am.
> YOU: No.

My point, if not already obvious, is that Sal doesn't need the grey suit and blue tie to be Sal. There might be more to him than you know, and perhaps the red sweat pants and Metallica shirt express his personality better than the suit, which he only wore because he thought you liked it better, or because that's just what he did on Thursday nights.

Even a simple thing can be seen from many different angles. A cube seen from the side may appear to be a square, but move over to the right and upward, and it will appear as a diamond. A square drawn on a flat plane looks like a line if the person looking is on the same plane. A line looked at from one side looks like a line, but from another side looks like a single point. Even a point, when viewed relatively next to another object, can look closer or farther away from it depending on the angle it is viewed at, and if you look at the point parallel to a line behind it, it completely disappears.

This applies to human beings as well, and everything

else in existence. Depending on how you look at it, anything can appear very differently depending on your viewpoint. But that doesn't change the fact that the cube is one and the same cube, no matter what angle you look at it from, and the square one and the same square, and so on with the line, the point, and everyone and everything in your life, including your friend Sal. And the fact that you may never have seen him in sweat pants doesn't change the fact that it's still the same old Sal.

The God of traditional theism is a Mind of utter simplicity. This is the only way to honestly account for the motion we find in the world, the causality, the necessity of its forces, its goodness and its order, as well as the only way to really answer the question: "Where did the universe come from?" The farther back we trace all these things, the simpler the story gets, until we get to something simpler than any of the forces of nature and more powerful than the Big Bang, something outside space and time and therefore without location or duration, something unchanging and therefore needing nothing before it to explain it.

But just like the super-simple geometrical point I mentioned above, this utterly simple God can be viewed from an infinite variety of angles. The angle that we've been pursuing has been what we can discover with unaided human reason. It's no surprise that our conclusions bear a striking resemblance to the God of the deists: this is the only aspect of God that reason can find on its own. But it is God nevertheless. Unfortunately, the New Atheists tend to confuse this concept as much as they confuse the concept of "nothing."

In the end, the heart of the fallacy utilized by the New Atheism is the following: "Arguments for a First Cause don't prove a Personal God. I think 'God' should only refer to a Personal God. Therefore, there is no God." Again, it comes down to a confusion of terms, and a confusion of questions. Whether there is a God, what we know of God based on the proofs for his existence, whether or not this God is personal or is the same as that of some particular religion, are all absolutely different questions. When he's being clear with his terms, Dawkins basically admits that he believes in God:

> Dyson could easily refute the implication of these quotations from his Templeton acceptance speech, if only he would explain clearly what evidence he finds to believe in God, in something more than just the Einsteinian sense which, as I explained in Chapter 1, we can all trivially subscribe to.[1]

Krauss admits to being unable to "rule out" the Deistic God (what Dawkins above calls "Einsteinian"):

> The apparent logical necessity of First Cause is a real issue for any universe that has a beginning. Therefore, on the basis of logic alone one cannot rule out such a deistic view of nature. But even in this case it is vital to realize that this deity bears no logical connection to the personal deities of the world's great religions, in spite of the fact that it is often used to justify them.[2]

This last claim, that the First Cause bears "no logical con- nection to the personal deities of the world's great religions" is exactly the heart of the question.

While I'm refreshed by the honesty of Dawkins and

---

[1]   Dawkins, *The God Delusion*, 183.
[2]   Krauss, *A Universe from Nothing*, 173.

Krauss in admitting that, at the very least, the Creator-God of the proofs of Aquinas, or certainly the God of deism, isn't abhorrent to reason, it seems they drop the ball again when it comes to the God of religion:

> Time and time again, my theologian friends returned to the point that there had to be a reason why there is something rather than nothing. There must have been a first cause of everything, and we might as well give it the name God. Yes, I said, but it must have been simple and therefore, whatever else we call it, God is not an appropriate name (unless we very explicitly divest it of all the baggage that the word "God" carries in the minds of most religious believers).[3]

The problem here is that the logical order is reversed. Dennett makes the same mistake a little more obviously:

> All that is left over in need of explanation at this point is a certain perceived elegance or wonderfulness in the observed laws of physics. If you doubt that the hypothesis of an infinity of variant universes could actually explain this elegance, you should reflect that this has at least as much claim to being a non-question-begging explanation as any traditional alternative; by the time God has been depersonalized to the point of being some abstract and timeless principle of beauty or goodness, it is hard to see how the existence of God could explain anything.[4]

---

[3] Dawkins, *The God Delusion*, 184–185.
[4] Dennett, *Darwin's Dangerous Idea*, 180.

It's not at all that God has been "depersonalized." It's that God has been discovered. What kind of Personality he might have is a secondary question. The fact that there is no pattern in the Cosmic Microwave Background radiation that spells out "Yahweh" shouldn't bother anyone of any faith. Perhaps the First Cause and the Origin of the Big Bang and the Laws of Nature is an impersonal, uncaring, unloving immaterial Force that couldn't care less about us or anything else it made. Perhaps he's a loving Father who sent his Son to die for our sins. Perhaps he's an elephant riding a tiny mouse (he's not). But it's wrong to try to answer the second question without admitting an answer to the first. There is a God. Only after agreeing on this can we even begin to ask the question, "Now what kind of God is it reasonable to expect?"

Blaise Pascal, a more ardent Catholic than Descartes and someone more abused by the Church than Galileo, famously distinguished the God he encountered during a mysterious, mystical experience he had on November 23, 1654, from "the God of the philosophers." I'll quote this passage in full here, because it's interesting in many different ways. This was apparently hand-written by Pascal and sewn into the lining of one of his garments, so that it would always be near him. It was found only after his death. Here's what it says:

> The year of grace 1654, Monday, 23 November, day of St. Clement, Pope and Martyr. From about half-past ten in the evening until about half-past twelve, midnight, FIRE. God of Abraham, God of Isaac, God of Jacob, not of the philosophers nor of the Wise. Assurance, joy, assurance, feeling, joy, peace. . . . Just Father, the world has not known

thee but I have known thee. Joy, joy, joy, tears of joy.[5]

Intense, to say the least. But the question I'd ask Pascal if I could is this: Why *isn't* this the "God of the philosophers?"

Let's take Aristotle as an example. This is a philosopher with no access to any Judeo-Christian Scripture such that Pascal would have been familiar with ("God of Abraham, Isaac, and Jacob"). Moreover, it's pretty clear from Aristotle's writings that he saw religion as a useful instrument of the State, but nothing more, and certainly nothing describing the reality of any real god or gods. In Part 7 of Book XII of his *Metaphysics*, Aristotle describes the God he believes he has just proven: "We say therefore that God is a living being, eternal, most good, so that life and duration continuous and eternal belong to God; for this is God."[6] Earlier on he showed that his Final Cause (that is, the Ultimate Purpose of the universe) is a perfect Mind which moves by "being loved;"[7] he shows how "the unmovable First Mover is One both in definition and in number;"[8] he associates this God with perfect beauty and goodness and order. I won't quote everything because you should really read Aristotle for yourself. Don't listen to those who disparage philosophy; give it a real shot. There is little better you could do with your time.

This is the "God of the philosophers." What's missing? Well, the thing about Aristotle's God is that he only seems to ever think about himself—"Thought thinking about thinking" is the most succinct description of Aristotle's

[5] Blaise Pascal, "The Memorial," trans. A. J. Krailsheimer (London: Penguin Books, 1986), 309.
[6] Aristotle *Metaphysics* XII, pt. 7.
[7] Ibid.
[8] Ibid., pt. 8.

God. So he doesn't think about us, and busies himself by being thoughtfulness itself, immaterial and infinitely powerful, and being so lovable and good that the secondary movers (perhaps Aristotle's name for the forces of nature) do their thing by trying to be like him and share in his life. Aristotle's God isn't far removed from the God of the deists. What's missing from the God of the philosophers is interaction with humanity. This is probably what Pascal meant.

But that's not to say that the God discoverable by reason is something different than the personal God of religion. It could be that these are just two different aspects of this one perfect Being. It's a logical mess to think that Sal can only be Sal if he's wearing the suit and tie you're used to. I can't speak for every religion here, but Catholic theology understands that the God revealed in the Scriptures is a deeper aspect of one and the same God working in nature discoverable by reason. If he is shown to have some qualities that aren't discoverable by reason alone, that doesn't mean he's a different God any more than Sal's t-shirt means it's a different Sal. It just means that we're getting to know him more personally, rather than only the stiff, formal way we knew him before.

Deism isn't an isolation of the God discoverable by reason; it's a denial that this God *could* be anything more. That God began the world and works through natural forces is (to me, at least) clear beyond any doubt. But that he *cannot* interact differently with his creation, or does not, or has not, is an entirely different claim. In this case, deism requires the examination and falsification of every religion before it is reasonably proven. But barring that, the internal logic of deism seems backwards. That there is a God who is outside time and space who created both, but who did so for no reason and cares nothing about anything he made, is an incongruous claim at least. That the God who used infinite power to create the world from nothing, the Mind who brought forth the forces of nature so precisely, should in fact care for the world he made, and especially for those creatures who have minds of their own, seems by far the more reasonable claim, all things considered.

Somebody's Right

Even assuming that theism is true (there is a God) and that deism is incongruous (it would be odd for God not to interact with the world after creating it), that doesn't really help one very far along the path of finding out which of the religions, if any, is the right one. In fact, it's exactly here that the question becomes messiest. If there is a God, and it is not unreasonable to believe that this God somehow interacts with the human race, then how are we to know which God is the right one, when there are so many options? Every religion, by definition, claims to have had some conversation or another with some God or another. How can one sift through so many contradictory possibilities, when more religions or religious sects pop up every day?

I can very much understand the temptation to just forget the whole thing and scrap the whole idea of religion. But this is excessively impatient, and questions as big as the whole universe deserve more of our time than that if we are going to consider ourselves reasonable human beings. Unless you've made a serious effort examining individual religions in their own words, dismissing them all is not a reasonable conclusion. The same goes for the "all religions teach the same thing" philosophy. Unless you know something substantial about every single religion out there, that's a jump in reasoning. It's quite possible that some religions teach very similar things, and quite possible that they don't. You need to do your research before you make any such conclusion, and your research needs to be more than reading a bumper sticker or an introductory college textbook.

This is another place where you're going to find me agreeing more with the New Atheism authors than with almost anyone else. I believe religion must be examined critically by reason, and that if reason isn't our starting point and our common ground as human beings, we are begging for disaster. I happen to disagree with the reasoning of the New Atheists, but at least they are attempting to reason with what I assume is a real desire to know the truth. I'm sad to say that I don't think I can make that same assumption when it comes to many adherents of many religions. Some religious sects are essentially founded on a rejection of reason. Luther famously called reason a "whore," and some medieval Muslim philosophers, in what seemed an act of desperation, declared that there were in fact two distinct "truths," one of religion and one of reason. I'm not sure what this implies, but it's certainly odd. I am not apologetic or sorry for saying this: the moment reason is rejected, humanity is lost; and so, any religion that rejects reason should be rejected for that very reason, by any reasonable human being.

It is a fatal oversimplification, however, to assume that all religions reject reason because some of them do. Luther's rejection of reason was an act of rebellion against the Catholic tradition. This is one of the reasons I find it deeply ironic when Luther is presented as a liberal free-thinker while Thomas Aquinas, who dedicated his life to reasonable discourse, is shown as a stuffy, thoughtless dogmatist, or when the Protestant churches are seen as rational and humanistic, while one of the big reasons the Catholic

Church condemned them as heretical was because of their rejection of reason and philosophy.

The Unbelievers, a movie more about the supposed heroism of Richard Dawkins and Lawrence Krauss than about atheism, begins with a series of statements from different members of the New Atheist group and celebrities of like mind (contrast this with Aquinas beginning every article of his *Summa* with "Objections" from those who disagree with him). During this opening montage, comedian Ricky Gervais makes what he seems to think a bold statement: "Facts, if you're rational, should change your beliefs."[9] Though he acts as if he is speaking in defiance of all human history, this is something everyone should agree with. On the one hand, I can understand why an atheist might consider this a controversial statement in the eyes of some religions. On the other hand, I think someone making a movie professing to be about the belief in God should do his research before implying that religious people as such would object to this.

Yes, evidence should change our minds. Yes, reason should guide our beliefs (that is, in fact, one of the first things I said in this book). Yes (to quote Sarah Silverman later in the opening montage), "everything should be questioned."[10] All this is only basic reasoning; it is something we should all share despite any disagreements down the road. I repeat that I can't blame the atheist for having the impression that some religions are against reason when that is true in so many cases. But I can blame him for generalizing all religions into a category comfortable to his

---

[9] Lawrence Krauss, JJC Films and Primordial Productions, *The Unbelievers*, film, directed by Gus Holwerda (2013; Los Angeles: JJC Films LLC, 2013.), DVD.

[10] Ibid.

own prejudices, and I blame him for this based on reason, not on faith. The facts simply prove him wrong, and so I can only assume Ricky Gervais will have the integrity to change his belief.

Again one prominent example among many is Thomas Aquinas: using reason, he debated thousands of questions for thousands of pages, compiling and examining every opposing viewpoint, weighing the strengths and weaknesses of all of them, placing those he disagreed with first and making sure he expressed their views correctly. He changed his mind on many questions during his life because he understood the opposing evidence better or discovered a new argument to support another viewpoint. He wrote enormous commentaries on Aristotle's works, and those of other thinkers. He is not alone among theist theologians in any of this—there are dozens of Christian saints as well as Muslim and Jewish thinkers who have done all of these things. Only someone utterly ignorant of religious history would think religion and reason can't go together. Despite all this, Ricky Gervais and Sarah Silverman are the ones chosen for the opening montage on a movie supposedly about religion.

Let me make a quick aside, while I'm already quoting *The Unbelievers*. A few seconds later in the same montage, Richard Dawkins recites these verses: "Science is wonderful. Science is beautiful. And religion is not wonderful. It's not beautiful. It gets in the way. There are all sorts of other things wrong with it but I mostly care about truth, the beauty of truth, the poetry of reality which is science and the fact that religion as a scientific explanation—it is a competing scientific explanation—it's so dull, it's so boring, it's so petty."[11] I hope it has already been made clear

---

[11] Ibid.

from the earlier chapters on the Big Bang and evolution that there is no reason to think science and religion are enemies. It's quite true that science and *some* religions are enemies, of course, but to say that validly about every religion requires inquiry into each one of them, not a sweeping generalization. The same goes for calling religion universally "dull," "boring," or "petty." Even if name-calling were included in rational discourse, it should be justified. I happen to think some religions are beautiful, interesting, and extremely deep, and yet even if taste in such things were objective, being dull, boring, and petty wouldn't make anything untrue.

I'm not going to try and prove which religion is the right one. That's a different question entirely, and a different book, which I have no intention of writing. But it is a question that can and must be asked and answered by reason, and there shouldn't be anything else that takes reason's place—not prejudice, not upbringing, not emotion, not anything. It wouldn't be hard to guess which religion I happen to think reason justifies, but you need to reason through it for yourself. I'll just remind you to do it carefully, since there's a lot of confusion out there, and a lot of misinformation.

Let me justify something I just said: that the question of which religion, if any, is the right one shouldn't be answered by emotion. I said earlier in this section that I'd be agreeing with the New Atheists to a great degree, and here's one place where that applies. Sam Harris makes this point very nicely in *Letter to a Christian Nation*:

> I have no doubt that your acceptance of Christ coincided with some very positive changes in your life. Perhaps you now love other people in a way that you never imagined possible. You may even

experience feelings of bliss while praying. I do not wish to denigrate any of these experiences. I would point out, however, that billions of other human beings, in every time and place, have had similar experiences—but they had them while thinking about Krishna, or Allah, or the Buddha, while making art or music, or while contemplating the beauty of Nature.[12]

I couldn't have said this better. The question of religion isn't a question of what makes you feel good. All kinds of things can make you feel good, and quite often the things that can make you feel the best can be the most deceptive about reality (e.g., drugs or alcohol).

On the other hand, there are some religions that limit themselves to this kind of thing. Sam Harris's later book *Waking Up: A Guide to Spirituality without Religion* is an attempt to fuse some tenets of Buddhism with Atheism. Buddhism lends itself to this quite well, in fact, since it seems to make no claims about God or history as do the more Western religions of Judaism, Christianity and Islam. These religions, in addition to the spiritual and moral guidance offered in their teachings, make concrete claims about reality. It is these claims that deserve examination before dismissal, and just as with anything in life, this examination should be done thoughtfully. I should not dismiss any religion based on an oversimplification of it, or one (possibly misrepresentative) example of it. Let it speak for itself, and then examine its claims. That is real reasoning, and it leads me to my next point.

---

[12] Harris, *Letter to a Christian Nation*, 89.

PLEASE, TELL ME WHY I BELIEVE

Richard and Thomas were walking down a charming country road one afternoon, talking about life and all its twists and turns. A dip in the road caused Thomas to swerve his step, and he bumped shoulders with Richard. The pair continued to walk, and a few minutes after the incident, Richard brought up the shoulder bump:

RICHARD: I suppose I should ask what I need to apologize for, Thomas.

THOMAS: Why would you need to apologize, old friend?

RICHARD: I'm not sure. But a few minutes ago you clearly indicated how angry you are with me.

THOMAS: I'm sorry, I don't remember that.

RICHARD: Oh, it was indisputably clear.

THOMAS: What happened exactly?

RICHARD: You attacked me.

THOMAS: What?!

RICHARD: You assaulted me, mere minutes ago, and I would like to know what I did to provoke such wrath in you.

THOMAS: I never attacked you! What are you talking about?

RICHARD: Look at your shoulder. There is a string of red fabric on it. That is the result of when you tackled me a few minutes ago. I suppose this has to do with your sister. I always felt tension from you when I dated her in high school. It seems that all your anger is finally coming out.

THOMAS: I never minded that you dated my sister! And that was ten years ago!

RICHARD: Yet, the fact is that you assaulted me. I
see no other explanation for this.

THOMAS: I bumped into you because there was a
dip in the road and I lost my step!

RICHARD: No.

The "fact" is, Thomas bumped into Richard. The interpretation of the fact is an entirely different story. Why
Thomas dunnit is different than the fact he dunnit, and
while it's possible that he has subconsciously harbored feelings of resentment against Richard for a decade and that
they only came out during this afternoon walk in the form
of a shoulder bump, it's likely that Thomas would understand his own intentions better than Richard would.

I am convinced by the proofs I presented in chapter
three, as well as the rest of the material I have written about
in this book. That's the reason I wrote it. If you think the
reasoning is bad or that I've misunderstood something,
please tell me and I'll hear you out. That is all very reasonable, and I'd be happy to do it. But the minute you begin to
explain to me why I believe, you've lost me. I know why I
believe, and I've explained it. If you want to have a rational
discourse with me, that is your starting point.

I'm not dismissing the possibility of subconscious motivation. In fact, I strongly believe in it. I just don't think
it's a starting point for a rational discourse. It's possible
that someone might believe in God for some emotional
satisfaction or another, and there are plenty that would
admit that. At that point, the discussion on emotional satisfaction can begin. But when someone states their reasons
for believing something, and the response is, "No, that's
not why you believe; I'll tell you the real reason," that is
not the beginning of a rational discourse, but its end. Start
with the reasons stated, and discuss them. If there's some-

thing deeper down that's really motivating what someone is doing, it will come out. But until it does, pretending that you understand someone else's heart better than they do is arrogant and presumptuous. Let them speak for themselves, and take them for their word. That is basic respect, and it is required for any reasonable discussion.

Like I said, there are plenty of people who would admit they believe in God because it makes them feel good. At this point, I'd be the first to point out that this is not a good reason for belief. All kinds of things make you feel good. It doesn't mean they're true. To me, it doesn't even work on an emotional level—if you're afraid of death, why would you believe in hell to make yourself feel better? Nonexistence after death seems much less scary than divine judgment. If you're seeking comfort in life, why believe in a religion that (like mine) often asks you to become seriously uncomfortable—to "leave everything" and "deny yourself" and "take up your cross"? That seems like a terrible place to seek comfort.

On the other hand, it's possible that someone would choose not to believe in God in order to escape a guilty conscience; there's a story about Jean Paul Sartre that indicates he did just that. But this whole thing is a silly game, and in the end none of it changes whether or not some religion is true or false. If someone believes in God for an emotional reason, or disbelieves for an equally emotional one, it doesn't affect the question in any way. The question of God's existence doesn't depend on the interior motivation of anyone. Neither do questions about Moses, Jesus, or Mohammed.

Unfortunately, many people seem to have a great time explaining to others why they believe what they believe. Here are three examples from three of the big names we've seen already. First, Bertrand Russell shares his feelings on the matter:

As I said before, I do not think that the real reason why people accept religion has anything to do with argumentation. They accept religion on emotional grounds.[13]

Christopher Hitchens specifies the driving emotion behind religion as fear, and specifically fear of death:

Religious faith is, precisely *because* we are still-evolving creatures, ineradicable. It will never die out, or at least not until we get over our fear of death, and of the dark, and of the unknown, and of each other.[14]

Richard Dawkins is more cautious, and gives several options:

Everybody has their own pet theory of where religion comes from and why all human cultures have it. It gives consolation and comfort. It fosters togetherness in groups. It satisfies our yearning to understand why we exist.[15]

Of course, there are many possibilities for the interior motivations of people who practice religion. It's very possible that many believe out of fear of death, or out of a wish to belong, or for a hundred other reasons. There might be parallel reasons someone might become an atheist. I've met people who admitted doing so for the purpose of looking

---

[13] Russell, "The Emotional Factor" in *Why I Am Not a Christian*, 19.
[14] Christopher Hitchens, "Putting it Mildly" in *God is Not Great: How Religion Poisons Everything* (New York: Twelve, 2009), 12.
[15] Dawkins, *The God Delusion*, 190.

smart to others. That doesn't disprove atheism any more than someone believing in God to feel less afraid of death disproves theism. The whole enterprise is a waste of words, and a distraction from the heart of the argument.

What Religion Causes: Calm Down Again

It's amazing to me how unscientific some scientists can be. A basic education teaches us that establishing causality is extremely difficult, and that it's very easy to be wrong if you're not careful. Potential medicines are tested carefully against placebos during experiments to verify that the substance itself, rather than some psychosomatic effect, is producing the desired result. John Stuart Mill came up with five "Methods to Discover Causality."[16] Here they are, with some examples I came up with for my basic Logic course, partially inspired by *The Simpsons*:

1. Direct Method of Agreement
"If two or more instances of the phenomenon under investigation have only one circumstance in common, the circumstance in which alone all the instances agree, is the cause (or effect) of the given phenomenon."

All the people working at the nuclear power plant have cancer, and only they do, and the only difference between them and everyone else is the radiation they live with. The radiation must be causing the cancer.

---

[16] All of the methods come from John Stuart Mill's *A System of Logic: Ratiocinative and Inductive, Being a Connected View of the Principles of Evidence, and the Methods of Scientific Investigation* (Cambridge, England: Cambridge University Press, 2011).

2. Method of Difference

"If an instance in which the phenomenon under investigation occurs, and an instance in which it does not occur, have every circumstance in common save one, that one occurring only in the former; the circumstance in which alone the two instances differ, is the effect, or the cause, or an indispensable part of the cause, of the phenomenon."

The people working at the Springfield power plant are getting cancer, but not those in Shelbyville. The only difference is that the Shelbyville plant workers eat White Castle hamburgers. White Castle hamburgers must prevent cancer.

3. Joint Method of Agreement and Difference

"If two or more instances in which the phenomenon occurs have only one circumstance in common, while two or more instances in which it does not occur have nothing in common save the absence of that circumstance: the circumstance in which alone the two sets of instances differ, is the effect, or cause, or a necessary part of the cause, of the phenomenon."

We gave the Springfield plant workers White Castle hamburgers, and they immediately stopped getting cancer.

4. Method of Residues

"Deduct from any phenomenon such part as is known by previous inductions to be the effect of certain antecedents, and the residue of the phenomenon is the effect of the remaining antecedents."

A balloon is heavier when it is full; air must therefore have weight.

5. Method of Concomitant Variations

"Whatever phenomenon varies in any manner whenever another phenomenon varies in some particular manner, is either a cause or an effect of that phenomenon, or is connected with it through some fact of causation."

Pipe smoking is linked to longer life since statistically pipe smokers live longer than non-smokers.

Notice how careful Mill's language is, over and over again: just because two things are found together doesn't mean the one you think is a cause really is the cause. It might be an effect, or both might be caused by the same thing that is unknown to you, or that you just haven't thought about yet. And just because some sequence of events makes sense to you doesn't mean that's really the way things are.

Contrast this careful treading with basically any of the New Atheism thinkers. Let's start with Bertrand Russell, whose logic should really be better:

Religion is based, I think, primarily and mainly upon fear. It is partly the terror of the unknown and partly, as I have said, the wish to feel that you have a kind of elder brother who will stand by you in all your troubles and disputes. Fear is the basis of the whole thing—fear of the mysterious, fear of defeat, fear of death. Fear is the parent of cruelty, and therefore it is no wonder if cruelty and religion have gone hand in hand.[17]

This is a double fallacy. He makes the genetic fallacy I discussed in the last section when he tells believers why they

---

[17] Russell, "Fear, the Foundation of Religion" in *Why I Am Not a Christian*, 22.

believe ("terror of the unknown"), but then he continues by explaining how fear causes cruelty. As I said in the last section, it's possible he's right in many instances, but making such huge generalizations isn't logical, and it isn't science.

Someone else who should really know better is David Hume, who spent a lifetime criticizing the logical leaps of philosophers and trying to prove that it's impossible to have any knowledge of causality at all. His mouthpiece for this worldview is his character Philo, whom we've met before, and it's more than a little ironic that this utter skeptic when it comes to metaphysics can make such bold and broad statements when it comes to religion:

> How happens it then, if vulgar superstition be so salutary to society, that all history abounds so much with accounts of its pernicious consequences on public affairs? Factions, civil wars, persecutions, sub-versions of government, oppression, slavery: these are the dismal consequences which always attend its prevalence over the minds of men. If the religious spirit be ever mentioned in any historical narration, we are sure to meet afterwards with a detail of the miseries which attend it. And no period of time can be happier or more prosperous than those in which it is never regarded or heard of.[18]

I could go on quoting writer after writer making the same broad generalizations. But let's say the facts of history are on their side. Let's say religion and war, oppression, cruelty, and so on, always seem to be found together. In fact, I'll go ahead and confirm that they are. That does not at all mean that religion causes any of these things. Go back up

---

[18] Hume, *Dialogues Concerning Natural Religion*, pt. XII.

to Mill's list and see if that claim checks out. It's more than possible that something else is going on. It's not that religion and cruelty are always in the same place because one causes the other. It's that they are both caused by the same thing: human nature. Part of us feels the need to worship something; part of us feels the need to harm others. Both of these effects are there wherever there are human beings. Saying religion, by its very nature, causes cruelty simply because the two of them are always together is as logical as saying breakfast causes cruelty.

But Hume's Philo makes a further claim—it's not just that religion and violence are always together; it's that religion and violence are always together in the same proportion. This is indeed a much stronger claim, but one that needs more evidence than the zero that Philo provides. Assuming someone has a perfectly objective reading of history, as well as all the data possible (both of which are impossible), an argument for this could be made, in which case something might be said about religion, or some particular religion. But a sweeping statement like "more religion = more cruelty" is closer to a bumper sticker than to science. More likely is the sweeping statement "more religion = more universities and hospitals," both of these having been introduced to Europe through the Catholic Church. Nor are they, like war and cruelty, found in every culture. Religions didn't invent murder or oppression. But I'm not naïve. Religion may not cause cruelty by its very nature, but some religions might. Yet again, this is where the question requires us to do our homework.

On the other hand, other atheists (actually, sometimes the same ones) accuse religion of the opposite effect—not cruelty but passivity; not of oppression but slavishness. Nietzsche singles out Christianity for this criticism:

Christianity should not be beautified and embellished: it has waged deadly war against this higher type of man; it has placed all the basic instincts of this type under the ban; and out of these instincts it has distilled evil and the Evil One: the strong man as the typically reprehensible man, the "reprobate." Christianity has sided with all that is weak and base, with all failures; it has made an ideal of whatever contradicts the instinct of the strong life to preserve itself; it has corrupted the reason even of those strongest in spirit by teaching men to consider the supreme values of the spirit as something sinful, as something that leads into error—as temptations.[19]

At this point one wonders what religion is supposed to do. If it's vigorous, it's criticized as cruel; if it's peaceful, it's criticized as weak. Perhaps it's the critics that are skewed, not religion. This point is one I borrowed from a thinker named G. K. Chesterton, who might not be the most technical or rigorous thinker of the twentieth century, but is still among the most insightful.

But I need to make one final point before ending this section. It happens quite often that not only are religions found in the same place at the same time as cruelty, but they are explicitly named as reasons by the people administering the cruelty. Here I ask you to be consistent. Just as it's unreasonable to project your reasons why someone believes when they give you their own reasons, it's unreason-

---

[19] Friedrich Nietzsche, *The Antichrist*, from *The Portable Nietzsche*, ed. and trans. Walter Kaufmann (New York: Penguin Books, 1977), 571. *The Portable Nietzsche* includes Kaufmann's definitive translations of the complete and unabridged texts of Nietzsche's four major works: *Twilight of the Idols*, *The Antichrist*, *Nietzsche Contra Wagner*, and *Thus Spoke Zarathustra*.

able to deny it when someone flat-out admits his religion caused him to do something cruel. Yes, sometimes religion is used as an excuse for evil, and only covers up cruelty that would have been there anyway. But sometimes the shoe just fits.

MORALITY: OH.

This section might remind you of the earlier chapter on evolution, in that much of my criticism (and that of the intellectual tradition until the late Middle Ages) will be leveled against what would be called the "religious" side of the question today. Put simply, I don't think you need religion to understand what's right or wrong. I think you need reason. Again, just as with the evolution question, I'm not a radical in saying this—I'm as traditional as it gets.

In fact, the Bible teaches that you don't need the Bible to know right from wrong. Take, for example, St. Paul:

> For it is not the hearers of the law who are righteous before God, but the doers of the law who will be justified. When Gentiles who have not the law do by nature what the law requires, they are a law to themselves, even though they do not have the law. They show that what the law requires is written on their hearts, while their conscience also bears witness and their conflicting thoughts accuse or perhaps excuse them on that day when, according to my gospel, God judges the secrets of men by Christ Jesus. (Rom 2:13–16)

In other words, Pagans, who don't have access to the Old Testament, are able "by nature" to do what the "Law" requires. This is even bolder than what I said above. I said that we are able to *know* right from wrong without revealed religion; St. Paul is saying that the Pagans can *do* what is right without it, not only know it.

This may be, in fact, the most misrepresented element of traditional Christianity. People speak as if Moses invented morality, when nothing in the Bible indicates any such thing. Yes, laws and commandments were given, but nothing suggests that such laws were a surprise to anyone. It would be a monstrous thing indeed if Moses came down the mountain with "Thou shalt not kill" written on stone and the people were appalled, as if they'd never considered the idea. The Christian tradition sees such stone cutting as confirmation and clarification—a kind of explicit explanation so that nobody would have any confusion or excuse—not as a shocking revelation of new ideas.

So if Moses didn't invent morality, where did it come from? What is it all based on? Is it some set of arbitrary rules? Did God write every possible act on a wall and then throw darts from the other side of the room to decide which ones would be sins? Or is there some reason why some things are right and some are wrong?

Yes, there is a reason why right is right and wrong is wrong. No, it's not just an arbitrary set of rules. If that's what you ever thought, you've completely misunderstood the entire ethical teaching of traditional Christianity. I repeat, as I always do, that it might not be your fault because there are so many misrepresentations out there, and you might not have any idea how to sift through them all. But I've had great success simply going to the roots and letting the religion speak for itself.

What is the basis for morality? Let's see what Jesus thinks:

One sabbath he was going through the grainfields; and as they made their way his disciples began to pluck heads of grain. And the Pharisees said to him, "Look, why are they doing what is not lawful on the sabbath?" And he said to them, "Have you never read what David did, when he was in need and was hungry, he and those who were with him: how he entered the house of God, when Abi'athar was high priest, and ate the showbread, which it is not lawful for any but the priests to eat, and also gave it to those who were with him?" And he said to them, "The sabbath was made for man, not man for the sabbath; so the Son of man is lord even of the sabbath." (Mark 2:23–28)

The Pharisees see the Law (meaning here the Law of Moses) as an end in itself. We have to obey God because we have to obey God. The rules are the rules because he said so, and that's that. Not so for Jesus. For Jesus, the Law has a purpose. The Sabbath was made for man, not man for the Sabbath. God gave the law for us. We are the reason behind it, and the reason for it. Morality is based on the human being and his happiness, not on a coinflip.

So we can understand right and wrong through reason alone insofar as we can understand human happiness and what leads to it through reason alone. This is called, in the Catholic tradition, "Natural Law." In addition to this, for all those times we confuse ourselves, God (in the same tradition) steps in and clarifies things, and we have "Supernatural Law." But neither of these Laws are arbitrary rules in some cruel game; nor is God some score keeper waiting for us to trip up so he can collect his sweet vengeance when the game is over. These are the rules of a parent for his children for their own safety and happiness. He gave us the minds to figure it out, but he doesn't abandon us when we fail to do so.

This is a place where Aristotle and Christ have a lot in common. Ethics, for Aristotle, is the science of human happiness. That's his way of saying "the sabbath was made for man." Everything in Aristotle's understanding of ethics is fueled by this one goal in mind: what makes a human being really happy. Based on this, Aristotle (following Plato) notices that within us there is often a conflict between Reason and the Passions (his word for feelings or desires). His solution is for Reason to train the Passions to obey, and for the Passions to be refined so that obedience to Reason is easy and pleasant. His name for this is "Virtue." The opposite is "Vice," where the Passions call the shots so much that they blind Reason, and the result is addiction and ultimately self-destruction.

This has very little to do with religion, and anyone thinking clearly understands that doing whatever you feel won't get you very far, and that self-control is a good thing. If you can understand this, you can, on some level, understand the purpose behind every Commandment and every rule given by the Christian tradition. But that's another book.

In any case, it shouldn't surprise anybody when some non-religious person turns out to be a good person, a moral person, even a downright wonderful person. They have reason just like anybody else, and they might think more clearly and guide their actions more ethically than a lot of people in a lot of religions. Just because they aren't members of the particular type of religion you think is the right one doesn't mean they are, by that very fact, bloodthirsty monsters seeking to murder every baby they see simply for the sport of it. Christopher Hitchens points out a handful of morally exemplary atheists, ending with a military figure:

To look no further than the United States, the great Colonel Robert Ingersoll, who was the nation's leading advocate of unbelief until his death in 1899, maddened his opponents because he was a person of immense generosity, a loving and constant husband and father, a gallant officer, and the possessor of what Thomas Edison with pardonable exaggeration called "all the attributes of a perfect man."[20]

I would distinguish between finding the basis for morality in human nature, distinct from any particular religion, from finding morality in an atheistic world without God or purpose. It's one thing to say that natural happiness, and therefore moral rectitude, are possible outside some particular Church; it's another to say that either is possible, or has any meaning at all, in an empty and senseless world.

Perhaps this is why the New Atheists are more defensive than they need to be when they present their cases for morality apart from religion. Richard Dawkins goes to great lengths to present a case for a non-religious basis for morality, when, in the sense I explained above, he needs to look no further than the Christian tradition. He distinguishes between motives for goodness and standards for goodness:

> Rather, [the religious apologist's] claim is that, wherever the *motive* to be good comes from, without God there would be no standard for *deciding* what is good. We could each make up our own definition of good, and behave accordingly. Moral principles that are based only upon religion (as

---

[20] Hitchens, *God is Not Great*, 187.

opposed to, say, the "golden rule," which is often associated with religions but can be derived from elsewhere) may be called absolutist. Good is good and bad is bad, and we don't mess around deciding particular cases by whether, for example, somebody suffers. My religious apologist would claim that only religion can provide a basis for deciding what is good.[21]

I'm not sure religion is needed either for motivating someone toward good or for deciding it, and I don't think I'm alone in this.

There's no place I agree more with Dawkins than in the following paragraph, following the title "If There Is No God, Why Be Good?"

> Posed like that, the question sounds positively ignoble. When a religious person puts it to me in this way (and many of them do), my immediate temptation is to issue the following challenge: "Do you really mean to tell me the only reason you try to be good is to gain God's approval and reward, or to avoid his disapproval and punishment? That's not morality, that's just sucking up, apple-polishing, looking over your shoulder at the great surveillance camera in the sky, or the still small wiretap inside your head, monitoring your every move, even your every base thought." As Einstein said, "If people are good only because they fear punishment, and hope for reward, then we are a sorry lot indeed."[22]

---

[21] Dawkins, *The God Delusion*, 264.
[22] Dawkins, *The God Delusion*, 259.

I suppose such morality based on approval and reward is better than nothing, but it's certainly not ideal, and it's certainly a misunderstanding of at least one form of theism. If heaven exists, it's not an arbitrary reward for arbitrary deeds deemed "good" by an arbitrary God. Perhaps reward and punishment are useful for those struggling to overcome some lower desire so that reason may reign freely, but they are means to an end. The end of all true ethics is happiness.

It was an interesting moment in history when this principle in ethics was rejected. Yes, Plato's characters debate the issue in the *Republic*, but from his time till that of Aquinas we have a fairly consistent tradition basing ethics on happiness, which was understood as the fulfillment of human nature. It was Immanuel Kant who rejected this tradition and replaced happiness as the basis for morality with abstract concepts like his Categorical Imperative.

For someone who wrote a history of philosophy, Bertrand Russell has no excuse to misunderstand every part of this question:

There are a great many ways in which, at the present moment, the church, by its insistence upon what it chooses to call morality, inflicts upon all sorts of people undeserved and unnecessary suffering. And of course, as we know, it is in its major part an opponent still of progress and of improvement in all the ways that diminish suffering in the world, because it has chosen to label as morality a certain narrow set of rules of conduct which have nothing to do with human happiness; and when you say that this or that ought to be done because it would make for human happiness, they think that this has nothing to do with the matter at all. "What has human happiness to do with morals? The object of morals is not to make people happy."[23]

The irony of his supposed satire is almost sad.

Another type of accusation against religion is that it positively encourages immoral attitudes or behavior. I discussed this a bit in the last section regarding violence and cruelty, but it can be more complex than just that. Sam Harris accuses religion of instilling arrogance in the believer:

> There is, in fact, no worldview more reprehensible in its arrogance than that of a religious believer: *the creator of the universe takes an interest in me, approves of me, loves me, and will reward me after death; my current beliefs, drawn from scripture, will remain the best statement of the truth until the end of the world; everyone who disagrees with me will spend eternity in hell.* . . . An average Christian, in an average church, listening to an average Sunday sermon has achieved a level of arrogance simply unimaginable in scientific discourse—and there have been some extraordinarily arrogant scientists.[24]

This is another sweeping generalization, and what could easily be called a forced interpretation where there are many other possibilities. After all, while Judeo-Christianity affirms that the Creator cares, it also affirms that we are made from the dust. It is a much more complex picture than Harris makes it out to be, and oversimplifying the

---

[23] Bertrand Russell, "How the Churches Have Retarded Progress" in *Why I Am Not a Christian*, 21.

[24] Harris, *Letter to a Christian Nation*, 74–75.

psychological profile of religions with billions of adherents and thousands of years of history shows just how unscientific he can be.

Let me give another possible interpretation, from the perspective of a believer—that is, from someone who has actually experienced what Sam Harris pretends to understand from the outside. If the Creator cares about us, and created us with care, the internal response to this might not be arrogance so much as gratefulness. It might be something like a sense of dignity and self-esteem, and reverence for all the other creatures he also made and cares for. But you don't have to believe me. You can choose instead to take Sam Harris's word for what it feels like to believe in God. Just don't pretend you're being objective.

I suppose you could do the same for the atheistic worldview, and guess what it might feel like to believe that the universe is a black and empty world, meaningless and void of any purpose aside from what you force upon it yourself. You could even do some research on the matter and read Nietzsche and Sartre, or any number of existentialists, and actually support your contention with evidence. At that point, you would be doing much better philosophy than Sam Harris, but you'd still be wasting your time. It doesn't matter what I think atheism feels like, or what Sam Harris thinks theism feels like. It doesn't even matter what we think our own worldviews feel like. Our feelings don't define reality, and they don't answer the question at all.

Along the same lines, Christopher Hitchens, as anyone who has read him knows, has moments of great insight and clarity. Among them is this:

> The first thing to be said is that virtuous behavior by a believer is no proof at all of—indeed is not even an argument for—the truth of his belief.

I might, just for the sake of argument, act more charitably if I believed that Lord Buddha was born from a slit in his mother's side. But would not this make my charitable impulse dependent on something rather tenuous? By the same token, I do not say that if I catch a Buddhist priest stealing all the offerings left by the simple folk at his temple, Buddhism is thereby discredited.[25]

Indeed, Buddhism is not discredited by the stealing priest, nor is any other worldview discredited by any adherent doing anything; nor is it proven in the same way. But Hitchens loses this clarity, and falls into the same trap that Harris found, only a page later:

When priests go bad, they go very bad indeed, and commit crimes that would make the average sinner pale. One might prefer to attribute this to sexual repression than to the actual doctrines preached, but then one of the actual doctrines preached is sexual repression. . . . Thus the connection is unavoidable, and a litany of folkloric jokes have been told by all lay members of the church ever since religion began.[26]

As usual there is no statistic, no explanation of how such a connection works, no actual evidence of any causality between the "sexual repression" supposedly taught by the religion in question and the crimes of the priests under discussion. There is only a vague suggestion and an appeal to folklore. You're meant to fill in the gaps yourself. But as

---

[25] Hitchens, *God is Not Great*, 185.
[26] Ibid., 186.

usual the filling isn't there when you try to find it.

In honesty, of course, you don't need to look any further than Chaucer to see the folklore that Hitchens is talking about, but the interpretation that the religion somehow causes such infidelity to chastity is utterly backwards. Catholicism (like basically every religion and decent ethical system) says self-control and chastity are virtues. Blaming Catholicism when someone sins against those virtues is odd logic, to say the least. It might make more sense to blame an overwhelming worldview where self-control is a fringe concept at best, or one where chastity is positively shameful; or the weakness of human nature itself; or maybe it's best to blame the actual people who commit these crimes.

Such ideas are presented as if they prove or disprove some religion or another. I hope it's clear by now that there's no logic behind that. However, it would be interesting, as a side question, to see some actual studies done on the effect of religion on actions, or on personalities, or on happiness. For example, how much of a difference does it make for someone's self-esteem if they believe in a loving Creator versus a mechanistic, purposeless universe? Or is this more an effect of upbringing or caring parents? Or genetics? And how does this affect someone's behavior over the course of a lifetime, or the structure of society itself? I'm sure there have already been studies done on such questions, and they would be interesting to look at. But that, like so much else, is another question.

Politics: Ugh

While he has plenty to say about God, Aristotle doesn't have a lot to say about religion as such. It's significant that one of the few works in which he mentions it is his *Politics*. This passage, for example, is quite revealing:

> Women with child should also take care that their diet is not too sparing, and that they use sufficient exercise; which it will be easy for the legislator to effect if he commands them once every day to repair to the worship of the gods who are supposed to preside over matrimony.[27]

If you didn't catch it, Aristotle is advising politicians to make a law that pregnant women must go to the shrine of the gods of fertility every day so that they get exercise and have healthier pregnancies. Religion is, for Aristotle, a tool of the state. Where it would be too much work to convince everyone to do what's best (in fact, it might be downright impossible), use some religion to coax them into it, and the state gets the benefit without the effort. Plato has a lot to say about this as well, as do many other important thinkers whom I'll let you read for yourself.

This is a very common way to understand religion—"even if it's not true," the understanding goes, "it's useful." This was a more common conception in previous centuries, but the atrocities committed recently in the name of religion have made it a less popular idea, and illustrated with bloody clarity that religion (broadly speaking, if we make the oversimplification of lumping all religions together) can be as harmful as it ever was useful. It might encourage people to be kind, but it also makes people blow themselves up.

I hope I've already made it clear that this is a question that comes later. As far as the existence of God is con-

---

[27] Aristotle, *Politics* VII, pt. 16.

cerned, it doesn't matter whether or not religion is useful. The question is whether some particular religion is true. If it isn't, then (to quote Flannery O'Connor) "to hell with it," no matter how useful it may seem. But the world isn't as simple as that. We see (certainly in America, and with little doubt in most of the Middle East) the effects of religion on politics on a daily basis. I'm sure I'm not the only one who has the impression that some people would change the Apostle's Creed to say "I believe in One, Holy, Catholic, and Republican Church." I'm not sure if this attitude really wants to make the state an instrument of some religion, or, following Aristotle, wants to make religion an instrument of the state. As an American, I'm repulsed by the former, and as a Catholic, I consider the latter heresy.

While creating a practical Theocracy seems to be the goal of some, another extreme is to allow religion no voice whatsoever in the political world, even within the consciences of voters—"that's your personal belief, and it shouldn't affect public policy." I am of the opinion that both of these are oversimplifications that are harmful both to religion and to the state. I won't say much more about my political opinions (I rarely do); in fact, the central point of this section is to show the complexity of political questions and their interaction with religious beliefs, to show how the whole issue needs more thoughtfulness than we are used to giving it.

I'm not sure when exactly it became bad manners to discuss politics and religion in public, but I can guess that it probably came at a time when education in critical thinking was decreasing. Politics and religion are annoying topics because they are difficult topics. But the fact that they're annoying doesn't mean they are unimportant. One thing I happily admit about the New Atheists is that they've had a role in making religion again a topic people talk about and critique openly. Religion and politics should not be hidden secrets held fearfully behind closed doors. They should be openly discussed and debated, perhaps more than anything else, since these two topics seem to affect human lives more than anything else.

On the other hand, both politics and religion are often given unjustly cheap treatment when they are discussed. Enormously complex political issues are debated in minutes on television, implying to the viewer that whoever shouts the cleverest bumper-sticker slogans at the highest volume must be right. The same is done with religion. Public debates of this sort are worse than a waste of time—they are outright deceptive to anyone really seeking the truth. I regularly teach a seminar on Plato's *Republic*, where the idea of justice is discussed and debated for several hundred pages. Many people, including most of the New Atheists (barring, hopefully, Daniel Dennett), consider philosophy a waste of time, often for this very reason. But Plato didn't write the *Republic* so that people could have a quick and easy answer to the question of justice. He wrote it so people could think about justice. And perhaps people with a distaste for thinking rigorously and thoroughly about a question shouldn't be taken very seriously. Maybe they don't really deserve an opinion at all.

But even though it abbreviates things to the point of idiocy, at least the quick-draw debate discusses the issue. A complete abandonment of reasoning often comes in the form of "coexistence" or "tolerance." As I've said elsewhere, if by coexistence and tolerance you mean living together and disagreeing without killing or hating one another, I agree with you completely. But if you mean pretending that everyone really just believes the same thing deep down, or that belief doesn't affect someone's life, that is either incredibly naïve or incredibly lazy. This is where I think Dawkins gets it partially right:

> But what is so hard for us to understand is that—to repeat the point because it is so important—*these people actually believe what they say they believe.* The take-home message is that we should blame religion itself, not religious *extremism*—as though that were some kind of terrible perversion of real, decent religion. Voltaire got it right a long time ago: "Those who can make you believe absurdities can make you commit atrocities." So did Bertrand Russell: "Many people would sooner die than think. In fact they do."[28]

Oddly enough, the New Atheists and the Roman Catholic Church have something very deep in common. They both consider heresy (false belief) harmful to humanity. What they disagree on is what exactly the heresy is. But for both of these groups, believing something false can have serious consequences—not only in its "extremist" form, or only in exceptional circumstances, but simply in itself. It is the "militant" atheists who have the most in common with old-school religion. It's the watered-down religions and atheisms who would rather not discuss the issue at all, since it's impolite to make people think. To my observation, this is the final result of the "coexist" mentality.

If we're going to think, then we're going to disagree sometimes. And if we're going to disagree, we're going to debate, and then people with weak stomachs are going to feel uncomfortable and change the subject. I always like pointing out the character Cephalus in Plato's *Republic*,

---

[28] Dawkins, *The God Delusion*, 345.

the revered old man who claims to love debate and discussion, but who leaves the very minute the debate becomes intense. You need decently thick skin to think for long enough to get anywhere near the truth. But you also need some serious respect for your opponent, otherwise you'll misunderstand his argument and debate a straw man. In previous chapters I've shown how the New Atheists misunderstand the theistic side of the debate time and time again, although creating straw men is certainly not an activity limited to atheists—in fact, this is where people of all persuasions seem to coexist quite happily.

Teaching this kind of rational interaction—what used to be called, in Greek, *logos*—was the goal of education for much of both Western as well as Eastern Civilizations. But at some point, things changed, and education came to have a different meaning. I have yet to find anyone who says it better than Nietzsche: "What the 'higher schools' in Germany really achieve is a brutal training, designed to prepare huge numbers of young men, with as little loss of time as possible, to become usable, abusable, in government service."[29] Of course, his critique is not limited to Germany today, and I doubt it was in his day.

Yet again, I have to take a step back and affirm that I can't speak for every religion. The fact is, many, perhaps even most, religions are part of the problem and encourage people not to think (Cephalus, the character I mentioned above, had to suddenly leave the conversation in order to attend to religious sacrifices). This is not limited to religion, since all kinds of things in human society encourage us not to think, from governments to companies to news

---

[29] Friedrich Nietzsche, "What the Germans Lack" in *Twilight of the Idols*, para. 5, from *The Portable Nietzsche*, ed. and trans. Walter Kaufmann (New York: Penguin Books, 1977), 510.

channels to different forms of entertainment. Thinking is hard work, and lots of people will do pretty much anything to avoid it.

Of course, none of these institutions will come out and admit that they don't want you to think. There are plenty of other ways to say it. Some use words like "infidel," others label an idea "liberal" or "conservative," the New Atheists have lots of ways to stop their followers from thinking— just calling an idea "religious" or "unscientific" is enough most of the time, though when they're really stuck they usually resort to calling a question "uninteresting" or just changing the subject. Perhaps worst of all is the attitude of those I've met who seem to think that simply having read Dawkins and agreeing with him makes them *de facto* intelligent. Following Dawkins's Twitter feed, I wonder if he thinks that himself.

So what does all this have to do with politics? Everything. Politics involves many people, and anything that involves many people brings two facts along with it: 1) emotion, rather than reason, begins to take control the more people there are; 2) selfishness causes disagreements to become more and more violent.

How do you solve this problem? One possible solution is to create a totalitarian state that uses either lies or fear to keep everyone in submission; that way their emotions are held in check one way or another, and their selfishness at least can't hurt others. This solution is presented in Plato's *Republic* and is taken seriously by many thinkers such as Kant, Hobbes, and Marx. Most conceptions of a Theocracy would fit into this style of regime as well, where the religious leadership would call the shots; Capitalism fits right into this as well, as large businesses become louder and louder voices in political rule. Generally speaking, thinkers with a low estimation of human nature (they'd call them-

selves "realistic," and they might be right) end up endors-
ing this style of regime, whether socialist or facist, religious
or secular.

The other solution is much more difficult. Instead of
using emotional manipulation or ignorance to keep citi-
zens (the word in this case is being used very loosely) slavish
and in check, the state could encourage real freedom and
thoughtfulness through education. This was one of the
noble dreams of many Enlightenment thinkers, though
Aristotle considered such a thing as close to an ideal state
as we can hope for. The American state, among others, was
founded with goals similar to this in mind.

So I've gotten myself into another corner now: what
does all this have to do with religion? Unfortunately, quite
a bit. Religion, along with many other institutions, can
serve the role of short-circuiting the political arena and
often lends itself to the tyrannical aspects of the political state. This happens at exactly the same time religion
short-circuits thinking. Tyranny and ignorance are always
and everywhere the best of friends. I repeat that religion
has nothing even close to a monopoly on ignorance, and
that this economy is richly shared by much of the media,
most of politics, and sadly enough large parts of the educational system itself. But this book is about God, and
religion is about God, and so it's worthwhile to examine
some places where religion can really do some serious harm
in the political arena.

Dawkins brings up an example that shocked me to the
bones when I first heard of it in my twenties:

> Or, switching to Christianity, I could have cited
> those American "rapture" Christians whose pow-
> erful influence on American Middle Eastern policy
> is governed by their biblical belief that Israel has a

God-given right to all the lands of Palestine. Some rapture Christians go further and actually yearn for nuclear war because they interpret it as the "Armageddon" which, according to their bizarre but disturbingly popular interpretation of the book of Revelation, will hasten the Second Coming.[30]

I remember hearing of this a few years after I entered seminary—that there were Christians who were so excited about the Second Coming that they were attempting to *cause* it by supporting the state of Israel so that it would become strong enough to re-build the temple, so that the temple sacrifices could once more be offered in it, and . . . well, I lost track of the details, but you see my point. This becomes, believe it or not, an excuse to affect international politics. My initial thought as a naïve seminarian was that perhaps they had never read the numerous passages of the Gospels where Christ makes it clear that it's none of our damned business when he comes back, or that he couldn't care less about establishing an earthly kingdom, and that perhaps someone should point out those passages to the politicians/biblical scholars in question. I have since discovered that no amount of pointing can force some people to actually look.

Soon after, Dawkins quotes a journalist who discusses a similar dynamic in Islam, but who makes a further point:

The respected journalist Muriel Gray, writing in the (Glasgow) *Herald* on 24 July 2005, made a similar point, in this case with reference to the London bombings: "Everyone is being blamed, from the obvious villainous duo of George W. Bush

---

[30] Richard Dawkins, *The God Delusion*, 341–342.

and Tony Blair, to the inaction of Muslim "communities." But it has never been clearer that there is only one place to lay the blame and it has ever been thus. The cause of all this misery, mayhem, violence, terror and ignorance is of course religion itself, and if it seems ludicrous to have to state such an obvious reality, the fact is that the government and the media are doing a pretty good job of pretending that it isn't so."[31]

I have to disagree with Muriel Gray and Dawkins on this point, which they see as so obvious. The London bombings weren't harmful because they were religious. They were harmful because they were evil. The people who commit such acts do not commit them because they are religious, simply speaking. They commit them because they are stupid and evil. What role some particular religion has in refining their particular stupidity to such heights of evil is an enormously interesting question, but it is not one that will be answered by any kind of oversimplification. That is to walk down the same stupid road.

Using either religion or irreligion as a shortcut to thought is both lazy and harmful to society. Espousing one political ideology because people call it "scientific" is as ignorant as espousing another one because people call it "Christian." If either science or Christianity are worth a straw, there must be more to them than a political party. This is because political issues are, if nothing else, unbelievably complex, and such shortcuts only make a bigger mess of things.

Let's say, for example, some religions believe (as most do) that adultery is a sin. What this means for most re-

---

[31] Ibid., 343–344.

ligions is that the person who commits this act has done something wrong and is thereby disapproved in some way by his or her deity. This is a personal, moral issue, and no one is harmed, and perhaps many marriages saved, by this belief.

But it's not at all the same when we're talking about politics. Your religion might tell you that adultery is a sin, but that doesn't mean it should be illegal—your religion might not even say it should be illegal. Maybe it should, but there are lots of questions that need to be answered before you can make that case. The first is whether it's harmful to you as a human being as such, or whether your religion tells you it's wrong because it causes ritual impurity or for some other reason. If it's only about ritual impurity, then the heathen next door doesn't need to worry about it, and the state can leave it alone. But let's say it *is* harmful (I happen to think it's obvious that adultery is monstrous). Let's say it's harmful not only to you and your spouse but to others as well. That's the second question. But even that doesn't mean it needs to become illegal. A third question might go: "Should everything harmful be made illegal?" But this opens up a thousand other questions about, for example, the purpose of government and the limitations of law. And the whole thing becomes even messier when you happen to live in a society that contains many different religions and viewpoints, some of which might not even agree with your answer to the very first question.

The same oversimplification happens when the word "science" is thrown into political debates. In fact, everything ends up being the same except for the first question. Yes, let's say (as a random example) science has proven that cigarettes are harmful to the body and shorten life. That alone doesn't even prove that they are immoral, depending on whom you ask, and all the other questions remain un-answered—whether they hurt society, whether that means they must be made illegal, what the purpose of government is in the first place, and so on.

But worst of all, the element in politics that simply freezes thought in its place and paralyzes it utterly, is party polarization. I'm not sure how this affects other countries, but in America it seems like religious and political issues are written on small pieces of paper, thrown into a large bucket with some glue, pulled out at random, and those issues that are glued together are somehow irrevocably linked, never to be torn asunder. That's all the logic I can decipher in the American political process. If you're Christian, it means you must worship big business, disbelieve in global warming, and support the death penalty. If you're Atheist, it means you must be pro-abortion, pro-animal rights, and socialist. Penn Jillette is one good exception to the atheist mash-up of ideologies, and I'm not sure what connection there could possibly be between Christianity and big business, and that's exactly my point—there isn't. But unfortunately, you can walk into a Southern Baptist worship service or into a San Francisco art gallery and guess pretty precisely what most of the people you see there believe about most political issues.

This is unfortunate—no, it's terrible—because it shows a mental decay in our culture. If the questions "Is there a God?" and "Is there one God?" are distinct and need their own arguments, political questions need them all the more. "There is a God, therefore gay marriage should be illegal" does not follow any more than "There is no God, therefore the Bible should be banned from schools." This intellectual laziness, not religion, is the real opiate of the masses. Let me say this harshly, since those who need to hear it don't listen very often: Make the effort to make the whole case for every part of every issue, as the issue deserves and as your opponent deserves and as society deserves, or shut your mouth and stop poisoning the world.

c✘✘✘⁓

CONCLUSION

A CRISIS OF REASON

I'm never sure what to make of it when people claim things like "the world is going to hell in a handbasket." What are they comparing it to? The world when they were younger? But the eyes of youth might color things more pleasantly. It might not be the world that has gone to hell, but them. Or are they comparing it to some other period in history? But there are no objective historians, and whatever facts we find in books are filtered through imperfect human minds. And even with that filter in place, I'm not sure any other period in history was much better than ours, or much worse. The world very well might be going to hell in a handbasket, but it's never as clear to me as it seems to the person saying it. Even the subtitle of this book contains the phrase "an irrational age," but that's not to say there has ever been any other kind of age besides irrational.

Whatever the case, I'm quite sure it doesn't matter. Whether things were better a generation ago or not doesn't excuse us from facing the problems we have now. I haven't been around long enough to compare one generation to another, so I don't know if things were different before. But that doesn't stop me from seeing a problem, whether it has been there for a long time or not. The problem I see is that the world is having a crisis of reason. I choose this particular phrase to contrast it with a more common one—"crisis of faith." I don't think the world is having a crisis of faith. If anything, there is plenty of faith around, in both good and bad things. In some ways, there is altogether too much faith, and too little reason. Hence the real crisis we find ourselves in, at least to my imperfect eyes.

My objection to the New Atheists is not that they are faithless, but that they are irrational. I hope I have shown that in this book, and if I haven't, I'm hoping to learn the truth, one way or another. That's part of rationality—to be able to admit that you don't know everything. But as I've said over and over, nobody has a monopoly on irrationality. There is, evidently, plenty to go around.

The conflict in the world caused by our current crisis of reason is not between science and religion. And there's no inherent reason it needs to be between different religions. The conflict at the heart of human society is between reason and stupidity. If there is ever to be an escape from the ideological wars that have wreaked havoc with us through all of history, and very much so as well today, reason must win and stupidity lose. I'll quote Dawkins once more to illustrate a misunderstanding he reflects:

> Christianity, just as much as Islam, teaches children that unquestioned faith is a virtue. You don't have to make the case for what you believe. If somebody announces that it is part of his *faith*, the rest of society, whether of the same faith, or another, or of none, is obliged, by ingrained custom, to "respect" it without question; respect it until the day it manifests itself in a horrible massacre like the destruction of the World Trade Center, or the London or Madrid bombings. Then there is a great chorus of disownings, as clerics and "community leaders" (who elected *them*, by the way?) line up to explain

that this extremism is a perversion of the "true" faith. But how can there be a perversion of faith, if faith, lacking objective justification, doesn't have any demonstrable standard to pervert?[1]

No, Christianity doesn't teach that unquestioned faith is a virtue. Not until Luther, at least. Why do you think there was such a fierce fight during the Protestant Reformation? He made the whole Faith look bad. I can't speak for Luther, but I can recommend you read Augustine and Aquinas for a more accurate picture of how faith and reason are meant to interact, or John Paul II's *Fides et Ratio*.

But where Dawkins is right is that there is a problem with treating religious beliefs as if they are beyond criticism. This isn't only bad for public debate and freedom of speech, it's bad for religion. It's even worse for religious people, who end up becoming an organized group of sniveling whiners, or worse. An embarrassing example of this in America is the so-called "War on Christmas" that is supposedly waged every year. Nearly a century after Coca Cola began using Santa Claus for its advertising and decades after the song "Rudolph the Red-Nosed Reindeer" was composed, Christmas is, according to a group of bored bloggers, finally being destroyed by Starbucks and its red cups. Perhaps an actual challenge to Christmas might be healthy for Christianity. In the meantime, it might be good for all of us to stop being offended at everything; to stop looking for things to be offended by; to stop whining; stop avoiding the difficult questions; stop forcing our ignorance on others. It might be time to take the time to talk to others and convince them, or be convinced. Otherwise it might be best to stop talking altogether.

---

[1]   Dawkins, *The God Delusion*, 346.

SELECTED BIBLIOGRAPHY

*(Not a comprehensive list;
just the books on my desk right now)*

Barker, Dan. *Godless: How an Evangelical Preacher Became One of America's Leading Atheists.* Berkeley, California: Ulysses Press, 2008.

Boghossian, Peter. *A Manual for Creating Atheists.* Durham, North Carolina: Pitchstone, 2013.

Dawkins, Richard. *The Blind Watchmaker: Why the Evidence of Evolution Reveals a Universe Without Design.* New York: W. W. Norton, 1996.

———. *The God Delusion.* New York: Mariner, 2008.

Dennett, Daniel C. *Breaking the Spell: Religion as a Natural Phenomenon.* New York: Penguin Books, 2006.

———. *Darwin's Dangerous Idea.* New York: Simon & Schuster, 1995.

———. *Intuition Pumps and Other Tools for Thinking.* New York: W. W. Norton, 2013.

Everitt, Nicholas. *The Non-existence of God.* New York: Routledge, 2004.

Freud, Sigmund. *The Freud Reader.* Edited by Peter Gay. New York: W. W. Norton, 1989.

———. *Moses and Monotheism.* New York: Vintage Books, 1959.

Harris, Sam. *The End of Faith: Religion, Terror and the Future of Reason.* New York: W. W. Norton, 2004.

———. *Letter to a Christian Nation.* New York: Vintage Books, 2008.

Harrison, Guy P. *50 Reasons People Give for Believing in a God.* Amherst, NY: Prometheus Books, 2008.

Hawking, Stephen. *A Brief History of Time.* New York: Bantam Books, 1988.

Hawking, Stephen and Leonard Mlodinow. *The Grand Design.* New York: Bantam Books, 2010.

Hitchens, Christopher. *God is Not Great: How Religion Poisons Everything.* New York: Twelve, 2009.

———, ed. *The Portable Atheist: Essential Readings for the Nonbeliever.* Philadelphia: Da Capo Press, 2007.

Holt, Jim. *Why Does the World Exist: An Existential Detective Story.* New York: Liveright Publishing, 2012.

Hume, David. *Dialogues Concerning Natural Religion.* Edited by Popkin, Richard H. Indianapolis: Hackett, 1998.

Krauss, Lawrence. *A Universe from Nothing: Why There Is Something Rather than Nothing.* New York: Atria Paperback, 2012.

———. *Fear of Physics: A Guide for the Perplexed.* New York: Basic Books, 2007.

Leslie, John and Robert Lawrence Kuhn, eds. *The Mystery of Existence: Why is there Anything at All?* Malden, MA: Wiley-Blackwell, 2013.

Martin, Michael. *Atheism: A Philosophical Justification.* Philadelphia: Temple University Press, 1990.

———, ed. *The Cambridge Companion to Atheism.* New York: Cambridge University Press, 2007.

Martin, Michael and Ricki Monnier, eds. *The Impossibility of God.* Amherst, NY: Prometheus, 2003.

Nietzsche, Friedrich. *The Portable Nietzsche.* Edited by Walter Kaufmann. New York: Penguin Books, 1982.

Russell, Bertrand. *Why I Am Not a Christian, and Other Essays on Religion and Related Subjects.* New York: Touchstone, 1957.

Stenger, Victor. *God and the Folly of Faith: The Incompatibility of Science and Religion*. Amherst, New York: Prometheus Books, 2012.

―――. *God: The Failed Hypothesis: How Science Shows that God Does Not Exist*. Amherst, New York: Prometheus Books, 2008.

―――. *The New Atheism: Taking a Stand for Science and Reason*. Amherst, New York: Prometheus Books, 2009.